Soul Mentoring

Soul Mentoring

DISCOVER THE ANCIENT ART
OF CARING FOR OTHERS

David Robinson (signature)

David Robinson

Luke 24:31 (handwritten)

CASCADE *Books* · Eugene, Oregon

SOUL MENTORING
Discover the Ancient Art of Caring for Others

Copyright © 2015 David Robinson. All rights reserved. Except for brief quotations in critical publications or reviews, no part of this book may be reproduced in any manner without prior written permission from the publisher. Write: Permissions, Wipf and Stock Publishers, 199 W. 8th Ave., Suite 3, Eugene, OR 97401.

Cascade Books
An Imprint of Wipf and Stock Publishers
199 W. 8th Ave., Suite 3
Eugene, OR 97401

www.wipfandstock.com

ISBN 13: 978-1-4982-0115-5

Cataloging-in-Publication data:

Robinson, David.

    Soul mentoring : discover the ancient art of caring for others / David Robinson.

    xviii + 162 p.; 23 cm—Includes bibliographical references.

    ISBN 13: 978-1-4982-0115-5

    1. Spiritual Direction. 2. Gregory the Great. 3. Mentoring. I. Title.

BV5053 .R44 2015

Manufactured in the USA.

Dedicated to Robert Stephens (1932–2009)
soul mentor and friend,
and to mentors I've met with weekly
at Men's Prayer Breakfast since 1993.

Table of Contents

Preface: Caring for Feet

One of the most delightful experiences after a day of backpacking is taking off my boots and socks, and soaking my sore feet in a cool mountain lake. At the end of a day of walking or standing, our feet cry out for care. They are tired and need some attention. Learning to care for our feet is an essential part of our daily life. In the same manner, learning to care for the feet of others is an essential part of mentoring.

Why begin with feet? The ancient world understood the close connection between feet and the soul. Jesus took time to care for feet. "Then he poured water into a basin and began to wash the disciples' feet and to wipe them with the towel that was tied around him."[1] The occasion of Jesus washing his disciples' feet provided him with a teachable moment: "For I have set you an example, that you also should do as I have done to you."[2] More than physical washing of feet, Jesus called his followers to love others through acts of service, to come alongside others and mentor people by caring for them in practical ways. People have been doing this kind of "foot-washing" work for centuries, living out the ancient art of soul mentoring by caring for orphans and widows, picking up the dying off the streets of Calcutta, building hospitals and schools worldwide, and looking after people in their times of distress.

This book invites you into an ancient approach to caring for others based upon a book by Gregory the Great (AD 540–604), *Pastoral Care*, written as he began his service as pope in AD 590. The title Gregory chose to describe his vocation was *servus sevorum Dei*, or "servant of the servants of God." Gregory sought to serve those who were serving others. During his fourteen years in leadership, Gregory cared for mentors and took time to train them in the ancient art of soul mentoring. Much like the current

1. John 13:5. All Scripture quotations are from the New Revised Standard Version unless otherwise noted.

2. John 13:15.

Pope Francis, Gregory was a foot-washer, one who loved to stoop down to serve others, helping them in their journey of faith. His guidebook for learning the ancient art of soul mentoring invites readers to gently come alongside people and find practical ways to "wash their feet," thus caring for the tired, hurting, and neglected places deep within people's lives.

The design for this book follows Gregory's *Pastoral Care* chapter by chapter. For quotations from *Pastoral Care*, I've relied upon the latest translation by George E. Demacopoulos, published in 2007. I also reference three other English translations of Gregory's *Pastoral Care* and one Latin text of Gregory's classic work.[3] Throughout this work, I will refer to Gregory's book as *Pastoral Care*, though the footnotes will refer to Gregory's work as *Pastoral Rule*. I prefer the title translation *Pastoral Care*, as it dodges connotations of "rule" as law or regulation. I've sought to bring out Gregory's main metaphors, themes, and insights chapter by chapter, offering my own reflections upon Gregory's wisdom for mentoring in our world today. Gregory's writing is rich with metaphors, allegory, and symbolism, often drawn from the Bible. For example, in Part One, Gregory compares soul mentoring to an art studio, shepherding, a school, a cliff edge, lighting a candle, sailing in a storm, and an oasis in the desert.

At the same time, Gregory's writing can be difficult for the general reader today. Not only is his language from the late sixth century, but he also wrote specifically for clergy, those involved directly in pastoral care in their professional lives. Though Gregory's *Pastoral Care* was a classic text used widely across Europe for over a thousand years, today it is largely overlooked or unknown. I hope in this book to reintroduce Gregory's *Pastoral Care* to a new generation of people seeking wisdom in caring for others. Very little of what we do in life has lasting results. By coming alongside people in a Gregorian way, we may discover the joy of being in touch with what is truly beautiful, artistic, and lasting: the soul of another person on life's journey.

---

3. All quotations from *Pastoral Care* by Gregory the Great are from the 2007 translation by George Demacopoulos, titled *The Book of Pastoral Rule*. I also referred to Gregory's *Pastoral Care* in three other English translations and one Latin edition, including: Davis, *Pastoral Care*; Barmby, *Post-Nicene Fathers*; and Bramley, *Regulae Pastoralis Liber*, with Latin and English translation presented side by side.

Acknowledgments

Though books are written mostly in solitude, I've never been truly alone, but surrounded by mentors who have helped shape my soul. I am grateful for the many people who have guided me along the path of soul mentoring, including: my parents, Don and Berta Robinson; my brothers, Doug, Mike, Jeff, Steve, and Tom; my grandparents; my parents-in-love, Bill and Sigrid Hudson; teachers and preachers; coaches and music directors; counselors and spiritual directors; professors and scholars; monks and priests; pastors and colleagues; seniors and children; elders and deacons; friends too many to name; saints, intercessors, encouragers, servants, caregivers, sisters and brothers in our faith community of Cannon Beach Community Church; our sons and daughters-in-love, Jonathan and Christina, Stefan and Jessica, and Thomas and Laura; and most significantly, my best friend and wife, Trina.

Introduction: When Setting out
on a Long Journey

In 1976, midway through my freshman year of university, I was struggling, confused, no longer sure of myself, and depressed. I seldom prayed, and avoided going to church. My mind was packed with uncertainties and unanswered questions about spiritual matters. One day in the university center, I bumped into Mike, a man I had met earlier in the year, during fall term. Mike was on staff with InterVarsity, a Christian group that mentors university students and faculty on college campuses around the world. After Mike saw the confused look on my face, he came alongside my life, sat down next to me, and asked me how I was doing. I told him I was feeling spiritually dried up. He didn't seem surprised, and he asked me if I'd like to meet once a week to talk about matters of the heart. I jumped at the chance. Every week for the rest of that school year, we met to go through a workbook on the spiritual life. I often neglected to do the homework, but that didn't bother Mike. He asked good questions and listened. He seemed very interested in my life, my doubts, and my questions. I've often thought of the gift Mike gave me that spring, the gift of soul mentoring. I still consider one-on-one soul mentoring one of the finest gifts we can give to others to make our world a better place.

Three decades later, during my studies for a doctor of ministry degree in Christian spiritual formation from Fuller Theological Seminary,[1] I discovered Johann von Staupitz (1460–1524), soul mentor to Martin Luther. After hearing Dr. Jim Bradley's lecture on Staupitz and Luther, a fellow student in our cohort asked me, "Who is your Staupitz?" I admitted I didn't have anyone mentoring my soul at the time. He admitted the same problem in his life as executive pastor of a large, growing church in the Midwest. We

1. My doctoral dissertation at Fuller Theological Seminary was published by Paraclete Press in 2010 under the title of *Ancient Paths: Discover Christian Formation the Benedictine Way.*

agreed that we'd hold each other accountable until we found our Staupitzes. Later that same year, Bob Stephens agreed to meet with me weekly to challenge me, hold me accountable, listen to me talk about my life, and pray for me. Bob became my Staupitz, serving weekly in that vital role in my life for several years until his death in 2009. Every Monday morning, I went over to Bob's house overlooking Haystack Rock and the Pacific Ocean. We drank coffee and talked about life and faith. Bob asked me about my marriage, ministry, and inner life. Each time we met, he prayed for me and also told me that he was praying for me the other days of the week. Few realize what a lonely road a pastor walks. Thanks be to God for Bob Stephens who walked that road with me as my soul mentor.

During that same course of doctoral studies at Fuller, I first bumped into Gregory's ancient classic book, *Pastoral Care*. In the pages ahead, we'll explore ancient wisdom for mentoring illuminated in this guidebook written fourteen centuries ago. *Soul Mentoring* invites you to enter a well-worn classic from the old world, *Pastoral Care*, written by Gregory the Great in 591.[2] By reflecting on this book on mentoring from the past, I hope Gregory will speak to us anew in the twenty-first century, offering guidance and encouragement on the spiritual path of mentoring and being mentored. In reading and studying *Pastoral Care*, I am convinced Gregory reveals ancient wisdom applicable to our time, both for mentors and those seeking to be mentored.

This book is intended for anyone who finds themselves alongside another human seeking guidance or wisdom, including counselors, mentors, teachers, pastors, and coaches, as well as those who are actively involved in informal mentoring. In addition, mentees, those seeking to be mentored, will also find Gregory's wisdom invaluable in pursuing such personal encouragement and spiritual formation. The terms "mentor" and "mentee" will be used throughout, with mentor referring to anyone who provides person-to-person care of souls and mentee referring to anyone who receives such care; the terms "soul mentoring" and "soul care" are used interchangeably. This book is written for both mentors and mentees, offering wisdom and practical guidance for both in spiritual formation.[3]

2. For more information on the life of Gregory the Great, see Appendix A: "The Life and Legacy of Gregory the Great."

3. The origin of the term mentor can be traced to a character in Greek mythology in the *Odyssey*. Modern usage of the term may be traced to the lead character, Mentor, in *Les Aventures de Telemaque,* by François Fénelon, published in 1699.

To some looking in from the outside, mentoring may seem easy. Gregory wrote in part to explain how difficult this work can be. There was a time when Gregory wanted to escape the burden of mentoring. He wrote to keep some from entering into this calling carelessly. Maybe this writing will prevent a few from blindly rushing into soul mentoring. Some reading this are already serving as mentors, but are looking for wisdom for walking alongside another. Others are looking for someone to come alongside their life to guide them.

Just as Gregory's *Pastoral Care* is divided into four parts, so this book is divided into four parts:

- Part One: The Journey into Mentoring;

- Part Two: The Character of a Mentor;

- Part Three: The Practice of Mentoring;

- Part Four or Conclusion: Care of the Soul of a Mentor.

When setting out on a long journey, we are wise to consider carefully how to best prepare ourselves for the road ahead, including what to pack and what challenges might lay along the road ahead. Gregory begins his *Pastoral Care* with words of caution to all who embark on the journey of mentoring. When Gregory first heard he had been elected to serve as the bishop of Rome in 590, he fled from the calling, knowing well the heavy burden of caring for souls. He withdrew from Rome to avoid the election, seeking to "flee the burdens of pastoral care," hiding in the contemplative life of the monastic cloister.[4]

Because of this personal crisis, Gregory opens his guidebook by warning people against rashly entering mentorship. Gregory was not the first to enter mentorship with fear and hesitation. Moses, Isaiah, Jeremiah, Ezekiel, Jonah, and Paul all experienced fear and inadequacy when called into service. Gregory stands in a long line of people who reluctantly responded to the call to serve as a mentor to others, knowing the heaviness of the burden inherent in that call. In the opening words of *Pastoral Care*, Gregory warns against rushing into soul care, describing this kind of life's work as a burdensome and precipitous venture before which we should tremble with fear at our inadequacy and infirmity.

As St. Paul readily admits, "But by the grace of God I am what I am, and his grace toward me has not been in vain."[5] By God's gift of grace, we

4. Gregory, *Pastoral Rule*, 27.

5. 1 Corinthians 15:10.

are called to mentor others, even in the face of an overwhelming sense of inadequacy. Looking back on my years in graduate school as I prepared for the ministry, I see a young man full of idealism and fear, feeling inadequate and underprepared to enter into full-time ministry. Like Gregory, I have always had a sense of hesitancy as I've walked alongside others, caring for their souls. My full name is David Gregory Robinson. When I became a Benedictine oblate at Mount Angel Abbey in February 2006, I took the name of Gregory as my oblate name, a name that comes from the Greek word *gregoros,* meaning "watchman." I've sought wisdom from Gregory the Great as a mentor and watchman in my ongoing spiritual journey.

By God's grace, we step out by faith along the journey into mentoring. By faith, we seek out mentors who can guide us along pathways of love. We do not begin on the first day in this calling fully equipped for the journey. We learn on the trail, growing, as Gregory tells us, "step by step". Like many before him and many who have come along since, Gregory hesitantly and humbly accepted the call to enter the journey of soul care, step by step, with fear and trembling. He is a reliable guide for both mentors and mentees on our shared journey into soul mentoring.

Part One

The Journey into Mentoring—
Learning the Art of Arts

O ver the past three decades, I've met with people weekly for informal mentoring. Over the first few meetings, we ask questions, share stories, and begin to get to know one another heart-to-heart. We offer one another something we both love, the essence of our very souls. For example, for several years, I met weekly with a young man now in his twenties. We began meeting while he was in high school. He taught me guitar; I taught him jazz piano. We shared our music as well as our souls. We spent time alongside each other conversing in music and in words, in silence and in prayers.

Mentoring is more about compassion and character than tools and techniques. Certainly, like any human endeavor, there are skills to learn and techniques to master. First though, there is a sense of compassion, the inner passion to step alongside the life of another human being to listen and learn, to love and be loved. Like a deep upwelling of spring water which overflows, creating a mountain stream, this call to compassion comes from the unknowable depths of the human soul, flowing out into the valley of another human soul.

Along this journey into mentoring we meet two people, mentor and mentee, walking side by side, sometimes looking into one another's eyes, trying to understand what can never truly be understood: the mystery of another soul. The beautiful character of all soul mentoring emerges from inner springs of humility, trust, and mutual vulnerability. When we have the integrity to admit we don't know, we are afraid, or we feel unloved, then the great work of mentoring can truly begin.

In the pages ahead, you will find my reflections upon St. Gregory's wisdom for soul mentoring. I follow his *Pastoral Care* chapter by chapter, as though holding up a mirror of Gregory's writings to see how they reflect on our century. At the end of each chapter in Part One and Part Two, I offer a "key to mentoring," summarizing the theme of the chapter for quick reference. At the end of each part, you'll find a mentoring inventory to help you personally engage in the themes and practices presented in that part. If this book encourages you to find a soul mentor or take up the call to mentor another, soul to soul, with compassion and character, then Gregory's wisdom will continue to live on in a new generation of mentors.

CHAPTER 1

The Art of Arts

Our family has greatly benefited from art teachers. After years of formal art studies by a variety of art teachers and professors, two of our three sons received university degrees in fine arts. The walls of our home are filled with original paintings and photographs by family and friends. Mentoring is an art. In one of the most beautiful phrases from *Pastoral Care*, Gregory describes mentoring as the "art of arts."[1] Gregory opens Part One with a simple truth: learn an art form before trying to teach it to another. In the same manner, we are wise to learn about soul mentoring by being mentored before we try to mentor someone else.

The troubles of the soul are more difficult to understand and heal than troubles of the body, "For who does not realize that the afflictions of the mind are more hidden than the internal wounds of the body?"[2] Yet some pretend to be experts in healing the soul, offering quick prescriptive advice for soul troubles, when they would never think of pretending to be a doctor or try to prescribe medicine for the body. For example, a friend of mine, who is a candymaker by trade, recently went online to get "ordained" as a minister so he could officiate at his cousin's wedding. I have yet to step behind his candy-making machine to attempt to handcraft saltwater taffy without the guidance of a master candymaker. Few would think the making of fine candy more difficult than the making of a fine marriage.

Gregory compares the work of mentoring to an art studio or a medical practice. In the ancient world, an apprentice would come under the care of a master artist, whether in painting or medical practice. Year after year, an apprentice was taught the disciplines, techniques, patterns, demands, limitations, and challenges of that art form. After years of intensive instruction from a master, the apprentice could consider taking on his or her own students, and begin to teach others what she had learned through experience

---

1. Gregory the Great likely drew upon the writings of Gregory of Nazianzus for the phrase "the art of arts." Cf. Gregory of Nazianzus, *Apology for his flight to Pontus*: "It seems to me that to rule men is the art of arts, and the science of sciences, for man is a being of diverse and manifold character." See Gregory of Nazianzus, *Apology*, Oration 2:16.

2 Gregory, *Pastoral Rule*, 29.

under the care of a master. In the Western world, the master-apprentice model for learning has largely been abandoned in the past few centuries, though this approach to mentoring has historic merit. What would a business, school, church, team, or group look like if every newbie was apprenticed to a master for a year? What if, after that first year of apprenticeship, the apprentices begin to take on students of their own, pouring their life and wisdom into other, younger apprentices?

There's grave danger awaiting those who presume to mentor others while stumbling in the dark themselves. As Jesus warned, "if one blind person guides another, both will fall into a pit."[3] Mentors are indeed eyes for others, looking to the path ahead and anticipating possible troubles. Soul mentors are people of vision who undertake leading others who are looking for guidance. When the guide's eyes are blinded by their own egos or fears or selfish pursuits, those they lead lose sight of the light along the path of growth and become burdened with weights they never expected to carry.

A thousand years ago, most training outside the home took place within the master-apprentice model. Over the past century, the work of mentoring has been entrusted to the academy, including universities and technical schools, where one master educator imparts specialized knowledge to a group of students. Often with little or no hands-on experience in mentoring others, students who graduate with a diploma are expected to be experts, including experts in mentoring others. The digital age of the internet has made it easier and easier to access training from a distance without the face-to-face labor of mentoring. Today, you can download a certificate of mastery off the internet and legally perform specialized tasks with that document, just as my candymaker friend did. Watch a few how-to videos on your laptop, register for your online diploma, and you too can become a doctor of souls.

Gregory calls our bluff. No one trusts a neurosurgeon who got his medical training from watching YouTube videos. The human soul, with all its wounds and troubles, is much more hidden and complex than the human body. We choose doctors who have worked long and hard to obtain medical degrees and experience before letting them prescribe our medicines or cut into our bodies. Why, then, are we so quick to accept the advice of a mentor who has little or no training? Today, we have access to a world of experts in every field. To whom do we look to learn the beautiful art of mentoring? As a wise spiritual physician, Gregory offers us ancient wisdom in curing

3. Matthew 15:14.

the human soul of many troubles. All who seek to offer such mentoring become people with eyes, with insight into the truth of the human soul, and with the experience to guide us on our inner journey of the spirit. When we lead others with our eyes closed, the blind are leading the blind, and we easily stumble into the pit. Better to seek out a person who has matured through faithful training in humility, wisdom, and love; a seasoned guide who can lead you along this illumined way of life.

Key to Mentoring

If mentoring is the "art of arts," apprentice your life to a master mentor, someone able to guide you with vision along your journey into mentoring.

CHAPTER 2

Good Drinking Water

The eight-mile hike to Hobbs Cabin in Tennessee took us all day under the hot summer sun. At ninety-five degrees and ninety percent humidity, the day quickly drained me. By the last mile, my friend and I were out of water, over-heated, and very thirsty. My friend assured me there was a great water source called Hobbs Spring next to the cabin. When we arrived, we found the spring fouled. The small, undrinkable pool of water at the spring was covered with an oily film. We spent an hour at sunset cleaning the spring, and then went to sleep thirsty, dreaming of mountain streams. In the morning, the spring had welled up with fresh, sweet water. We filled our water bottles for the hike out of the canyon, grateful for the gift of good drinking water.

That trip to Hobbs Cabin over twenty years ago taught me the importance of keeping my inner spring clean. How can mentors expect to refresh another person if their inner spring is trampled or fouled with impurities? The Good Shepherd described the heart as a spring of water, saying, "Those who drink of the water that I will give them will never be thirsty. The water that I will give will become in them a spring of water gushing up to eternal life. . . . Let anyone who is thirsty come to me, and let the one who believes in me drink. As the scripture has said, 'Out of the believer's heart shall flow rivers of living water.'"[4] Gregory draws upon this ancient metaphor of the soul, adding another picture from rural life, that of a shepherd caring for a flock of sheep. He writes,

> Just as when a shepherd walks on steep ground, the flock follows him to the precipice, so too the Lord, through the prophet, laments the contemptible knowledge of [mentors], saying: "When you drank the clearest water, you troubled the rest with your feet; and my sheep were nourished with that which you trampled with your feet and they drank that which your feet troubled."[5]

In this picture, mentoring involves leading people to a source of refreshment. Unwise, selfish mentors trample the water source, leaving a muddy mess for those they are attempting to serve. Some people spend years learning about mentoring, but trample over what they've learned by failing to live according to their own theories. The knowledge in their mind never moves to their soul or make a difference in their way of life. Years ago, I got to know the daughter of a best-selling author of parenting books. The author spent much more time writing, speaking, and promoting his books than he did caring for his own family, leaving behind an unhealthy legacy of neglect and resentment.

We are wise to pay attention to our manner of living and to the steps we take. Gregory calls us to grow into maturity in our personal life; lest we offer those we are mentoring a bad example with our muddied lifestyle. No one wants to drink from polluted springs. Our lives are like springs to those who come to us for refreshment. No one does more harm in mentoring than they who clothe themselves with an outward display of wisdom, yet inwardly are full of folly. Those who allow God's wisdom to well up within them, however, become a creative source of refreshment for others.

Nine centuries ago, St. Hildegard described the human soul renewed by God as "all verdant greening."[6] The greening of the human soul occurs when people have regular access to the source of life refreshment in God with the guidance of a wise mentor, an experience Hildegard describes as *viriditas*, the greening or rejuvenation of the human soul in communion

---

4. John 4:14; 7:37–38.

5. Gregory, *Pastoral Rule*, 31. Gregory quotes here from Ezekiel 34:18–19.

6. The Latin is *Viriditas*, meaning "greening" or "vitality." See Uhlein, *Meditations With Hildegard of Bingen*, 8.

with God. Constant J. Mews and Claire Renkin note that Hildegard drew upon the wisdom of St. Gregory from five centuries earlier, : "A key concept in her thinking was that of *viriditas,* the green life-force of divine origin that underpinned creation—a term that occurs no fewer than 56 times in [Gregory's] *Moralia* on Job."[7] Mentees are wise to draw on ancient wisdom for the greening of the soul by seeking out mentors whose lives are full of vitality like a verdant pastureland, and who have good drinking water of wisdom flowing from their inmost being to offer to all who are thirsty for refreshment.

I am a big fan of formal studies in mentoring, counseling, education, psychology, therapy, and pastoral care. Yet, in contrast with the previous chapter—which warns against seeking mentors without any formal training—in this chapter, Gregory warns against seeking mentors who only have formal training but no life character. Better to seek out a genuine person whose way of life matches their words, rather than someone with a list of formal degrees but very little life wisdom. Soul care flows out of a wise heart like fresh water from a mountain spring.

Key to Mentoring

Mentees are wise to draw upon ancient wisdom for the greening of the soul by seeking out mentors whose lives are full of vitality like a verdant pastureland.

CHAPTER 3

The School of Adversity

Think of the first day of school—maybe your first day of kindergarten, your freshman year of high school, or perhaps your first course in graduate school. Entering a new school involves adapting to new challenges and

7. Mews and Renkin, from their essay *The Legacy of Gregory the Great in the Latin West,* quoted in Bronwen, eds., *A Companion to Gregory the Great,* 334.

stresses. Stepping into a new school calls us into new ways of living and learning.

Gregory viewed life on this planet as being enrolled in a unique school in which we learn about ourselves and others through instructors such as Dr. Adversity, and her graduate teaching assistant, Ms. Suffering. As we have already said, a heavy load is placed upon the shoulders of those who mentor others. Those who are not yet ready to carry this burden will become overloaded from their unhealthy desire for recognition, and may lead others into unhealthy ways of living as well. Gregory points to Jesus of Nazareth, who continually gave of his life, entering into the pain and sufferings of others, to bring gifts of love, forgiveness, and mercy to all. Through his example, we may learn from adversity and brokenness, offering our lives to others in sacrificial love and compassion. Gregory calls this way of learning *adversitatis magisterio,* or "the school of adversity."[8]

Like children carrying books in backpacks on their way to school, so, all who mentor others shoulder burdens upon their backs. Gregory offers many warnings in the opening chapters of his book against entering this challenging work thoughtlessly or for the wrong reasons. There are plenty of burdens to carry in the school of adversity.

Examples abound today of celebrities and superstars who have made their mark on the world. Well-known people can push their way into our imaginations as living examples of fortune, fame, and freedom. These mirages hold out their lure, enticing us to seek entrance into the school of prosperity. Anyone who has spent any time reflecting upon the life of Jesus knows otherwise. He walked in our steps to show us the way to walk in his steps. As Peter wrote, "For to this you have been called, because Christ also suffered for you, leaving you an example, so that you should follow in his steps."[9] While there is nothing inherently wrong with fortune or fame, when we walk in the way of Christ, we are guided by such companions as simplicity, sacrifice, and service. The three classic monastic vows of poverty, chastity, and obedience present a counterculture alternative to the seductions of fortune, fame, and freedom. I suggest simplicity as an antidote to fortune (in place of poverty), sacrifice as an antidote to fame (in place of chastity), and service as an antidote to unlimited freedom (in place of obedience). These three instructors guide us in the school of adversity.

8 Gregory, *Pastoral Rule,* 33.

9. 1 Peter 2:21.

I remember reading an issue of Time magazine years ago that highlighted the lives of two famous men, Donald Trump and Millard Fuller.[10] Both were successful businessmen who had attained high levels of prosperity. While Trump continued to pile up his fortunes, in 1976, Fuller sacrificed his business career to enter the school of adversity among the poor, seeking to help them by building decent, no-interest, affordable homes. As founder of Habitat for Humanity, Millard Fuller began to help others by building homes for the poor. Through the gifts of thousands of volunteers, over the past three decades, Habitat for Humanity has built over 600,000 homes for 3,000,000 needy people worldwide.[11] During the weeks I've served as a Habitat for Humanity volunteer, I've personally experienced the joy of giving, building, and celebrating life together with others in the school of adversity.

Gregory invites all those who care for souls to enroll in the school of adversity. Those who have been trained to embrace the pain, suffering, and hardships of others know how to bring help and hope to hurting hearts. As Thomas à Kempis prayed,

> Write thy blessed name, O Lord, upon my heart, there to remain to indelibly engraven, that no prosperity, no adversity shall ever move me from thy love. Be thou to me a strong tower of defense, a comforter in tribulation, a deliverer in distress, a very present help in trouble, and a guide to heaven through the many temptations and dangers of this life. Amen.[12]

Key to Mentoring

To become a better mentor, enroll in the school of adversity and walk alongside another with compassion, willing to suffer with others who suffer.

10. *Time* 133, no. 3 (January 16, 1989).

11. For more information on Habitat for Humanity, see http://www.habitat.org/ (accessed on July 1, 2014).

12. Quoted in Job and Shawchuck, *Guide to Prayer*, 98–99.

CHAPTER 4

On the Edge

Anyone who has ever stood at the edge of a very high cliff understands viscerally what Gregory is talking about when he writes, "For no one who is imperfect should dare to seize a position of spiritual leadership, just as no one who staggers on level ground should set foot on a cliff."[13] Vertigo is a gift: it helps us keep our balance on the edge. While backpacking in national parks with my family, I've walked many times on narrow trails at the edges of cliffs. One wrong step would mean disaster and sometimes even death. At such a place, we take special care with our steps, keep our balance, and avoid unnecessary distractions. Soul mentoring is like walking with another person on the edge of a high cliff.

In his opening chapters, Gregory consistently warns readers of the many dangers inherent in mentoring and being mentored. One such danger is the neglect of one's own soul. While trying to focus our attention on the many challenges in the lives of others, we often foolishly overlook our own inner compass. How easily we lose our balance, overfilling our lives with external troubles at the expense of internal health and stability. A strange multitude of distractions lure us daily, leaving our minds in a muddle and our souls unstable. As a result, we are less able to walk without stumbling.

Sometimes I wonder what Gregory would think of our world today. Our lives are filled with electronic devices demanding our attention. Many of these gadgets connect us instantly with people we've never met around the world. For the first time in human history, we can hear the cries of millions of hurting people in real time around the world. We allow our eyes to become riveted to electronic screens showing us images of suffering as it unfolds. Never has there been a time in the history of the world when more people have been more overloaded with the knowledge of the cares of others.

Though we have access and even overexposure to millions of hurting lives around the world, we've never been busier. Multiple demands pull us in multiple directions simultaneously, leaving us with an inner sense

---

13. Gregory, *Pastoral Rule*, 36. *In precipiti* is the Latin phrase Gregory uses in this chapter, meaning "at the precipice," or on the edge of a cliff.

of stress, weariness, and compassion fatigue. When we are tired, we easily stumble; too many obstacles in the path and we're sure to fall.

The mind has difficulty maintaining balance when the soul is distracted by many matters. When we allow our lives to be led astray by outer distractions, we can lose our inner balance. We are wise to learn to stand on solid ground within our soul, rather than troubling our minds with many matters. We might compare such an overly troubled person to a pilgrim on a long journey who becomes so preoccupied with external cares that he forgets to check the map, and thus heads off in the wrong direction. When we neglect self-examination, we lose touch with our own souls and thus become less able to help others.

Just as our eyes and ears were designed to help us keep our balance while walking on the edge of a cliff, so our heart is designed to help us keep in balance on the edge of another person's life. Gregory encourages us to find our balance as mentors and mentees by taking time to examine our hearts. Soul examination leads to soul stability, and thus, a greater ability to keep our balance at the edge. Gregory reminds us to check our inner compass to better know the direction in which we are heading on our journey. This is especially true in the journey of soul care, a journey which is sometimes like walking on the edge of a precipice, requiring us to step carefully and keep our balance.

Key to Mentoring

Like walking on the edge of a precipice, mentoring calls us to keep our balance and focus our attention on the compass of the heart.

CHAPTER 5

This Little Light of Mine

One of the ten essentials for every backpacker hiking in the wilderness is a working flashlight with extra batteries. We use headlamps to keep our hands free for the tasks necessary at night, and we always carry extra batteries. One of my favorite times while camping in the high country is at night, when our tents glow from within with the light of headlamps as our family enjoys sharing stories, laughter, and memories from the day. On a recent camping trip, my headlamp went out while reading stories to the family, a problem quickly remedied by spare batteries.

People are given unique gifts, including character traits, natural talents, and spiritual gifts. The Greek word for gift, *charis,* generally refers to God's grace or favor, including the favor of receiving such abilities and talents as strength, musicality, intelligence, creativity, and love. Spiritual gifts, *charismata,* are unique spiritual abilities given by God to a person at the time of their spiritual birth or conversion. There are various spiritual gift inventories available to help a person discover their spiritual gifts. I have found the Hauck Spiritual Gift Inventory to be a helpful tool in mentoring people to better shine their light by discovering, developing, and deploying their spiritual gifts.[14] Such gifts are given for the common good, to benefit others' lives as well as our own. These gifts develop over time as we give ourselves away to serve others in love. In chapter five of Part One, Gregory offers a list of personal qualities for soul care, including integrity, self-control, wisdom, perseverance, responsibility, loving-kindness, and good judgment. Consider what difference such virtues would make in our homes, communities, businesses, or world if put into practice daily. Such qualities are like a candle in a dark room or like a headlamp in a darkened wilderness. We each have enough light to share with the people around us.

Gregory is concerned with those who hide their light, refusing to share their virtues and gifts. Gregory refers to a well-known parable of Jesus': "You are the light of the world. A city built on a hill cannot be hid. No one after lighting a lamp puts it under the bushel basket, but on the lampstand, and it gives light to all in the house."[15] We are encouraged to shine our light before others "so that they may see your good works and give glory to your Father in heaven."[16] Gregory encourages us not to hide our gifts and talents away, but rather to shine the light we've been given.

Those who neglect soul care are like those who live in a darkened room without light or love. At any moment, a lighted match may spark anew that inner light of love, and quicken into flame once again the intimate gift of soul care. Mentoring involves lighting the way for another

14. See www.stephenministries.org for more information on ordering this inventory.

15. Matthew 5:14–15.

16. Matthew 5:16.

person. We mentor others because we ourselves have been loved and seek to bring others into the light of love. As Robert Browning describes this beautiful moment in his poem *Meeting at Night*,

> A tap at the pane, the quick sharp scratch
> And blue spurt of a lighted match,
> And a voice less loud, thro' its joys and fears,
> Than the two hearts beating each to each![17]

Key to Mentoring

Like light from a lamp, we receive gifts from God not just for our own use, but to use for the benefit of others.

CHAPTER 6

Good Earth

We compost our plant and vegetable garbage in big cans in our backyard. We've done it for years. Twice a year, the two big garbage cans of compost begin to overflow. I turn the compost material over and see an abundance of earthworms doing their faithful work in the smelly mess. Every year, our organic garbage produces several wheel barrows of good earth, ready to be spread across our garden, bringing beauty by nourising our flowers, shrubs, and trees.

Humility, like good earth, or *humus*, is the soil of the human soul which is the source for all healthy human life.[18] Our lives are intended to produce beauty and fruitfulness in the lives of others. Our soul is like soil. Just as there are many kinds of soil, there are also many kinds of souls.[19]

---

17. Robert Browning, *Meeting at Night*, quoted in Aldington, *The Viking Book of Poetry of the English-Speaking World*, 887–888.

18. *Humus,* Latin for "good earth," is also the root of our English word for humility.

19. See Jesus's parable of the Sower, Matthew 13:3–9, 18–23. I draw upon this parable in this section.

There are some who withdraw from mentoring out of genuine humility, because they view themselves unworthy of helping others. When someone's inner life is full of the good earth of humility, they are ready to bring forth the health of new life and growth in the soul of another. When someone's inner life is full of the hard soil of obstinacy, they will not be able to bear fruit until they open their lives to God's grace which falls like rain.[20] Indeed, anyone who is truly humble is open to a life that is growing in love, able to receive God's good seed planted in their hearts and bring forth good fruit. At first, such a person may flee from mentoring others out of an initial sense of unworthiness. But after a time, with encouragement, they will overcome their shyness and find the courage to step into the lives of others, helping them find nourishment, goodness, and growth for their lives.

When we open our hearts to receive divine grace and truth, our lives are softened, planted, and transformed, able to bring forth fruitfulness in the lives of others. Some hardened souls are unable to receive the seed of divine wisdom, and thus remain fruitless in caring for the souls of others. Some souls initially receive God's seed, but are too shallow or too full of rocky soil. Though they initially spring to life with quick enthusiasm for soul care, they quickly wither and fade away when life heats up and troubles arrive. Some souls are choked by worries and desires, thus unable to bring forth good growth in the lives of others.

There are some who are ready to be mentored, possessing a humble heart and receptivity to inner growth. Yet because they are shy and nonassertive, they fail to find a mentor and do not enter into soul care. When looking for a mentor, seek out down-to-earth, receptive people who possess lives full of humus, the good earth of honesty, compassion, goodness, wisdom, integrity, and love. Such people are not perfect, but have allowed their lives to be transformed into good earth through the wonderful work of soul composting. Such people may at first be hesitant to mentor another. But with a little encouragement, they will respond willingly by stepping forward to help bring forth good fruit in the souls of others simply because they are confident that compost can be transformed into good earth.

---

20. I've inserted two scriptural images not found in Gregory's original chapter, both from the teachings of Jesus. First, hardened soil, referring to the first soil in the parable of the Sower from Matthew 13:3–9; and second, rain falling, referring to God's good will, drawing upon Jesus's teaching from Matthew 5:45, where Jesus teaches that God "sends rain on the righteous and the unrighteous."

Key to Mentoring

Humility, like good soil, is a sacred gift, able to bring forth the health of new life and growth in the soul of another.

CHAPTER 7

Heart Motives

One of the first great crossroads in the journey of soul care is heart motivation. What caused you to first seek out a mentor? Why did you get into mentoring to begin with? What drives you to step into the life of another to experience mentorship? What motivations will continue to strengthen you and guide you on the long journey of mentoring another person? Mentoring may be as informal as meeting with a friend or coworker over coffee, or it may involve years of training and preparation before entering into a mentoring vocation such as teaching, pastoral ministry, coaching, or counseling. In both cases, there are some who jump in quickly and some who withdraw at first before being drawn in.

Gregory loved writing about the active and contemplative ways of spiritual life. In his writing, he often drew upon stories that reveal these alternatives. Gregory wrote from his life experience. He immersed himself in the active life, first as prefect of Rome, and later as papal ambassador to Constantinople. Then he withdrew into the contemplative life of the monastic cloister. Finally, in AD 590, when elected to the office of bishop of Rome, he found himself called back into the active life of mentoring others as "servant of the servants of God." Gregory understood well the ancient prophets who were initially hesitant to enter into active soul care. He reminds us of Isaiah, Jeremiah, and Moses, who answered their calls to soul care with hesitations at first. Moses claimed he was unable to speak well enough. Isaiah lamented his unclean condition. Jeremiah believed himself unqualified for this work due to his youthful age.

Anyone entering into mentoring is wise to first examine their own soul and the motives of the heart. Moses was afraid when asked to lead others, though God encouraged him. Many wise leaders in ancient times were hesitant to take on the burden of mentoring. There are many today who can hardly bear their own burdens, let alone take on the cares and burdens of others.

Some enter into mentoring as a way to get attention, win favor, or improve their reputation. Such motives are not uncommon among those involved in full-time mentoring professions. Altruistic motives are often present in the hearts of those who serve in soul care professions, but can easily be overshadowed by a hunger for recognition, approval, or affirmation.

Others enter into mentoring out of fear, guilt, or shame. They seek to overcome these shadows by stepping into the light and offering themselves in service to others, hoping to exorcise demons of the past by acts of kindness in the present. Such motivations can get us into mentoring, but do not have sustaining power to keep us going year after year.

Still others are truly gifted and called to serve in full-time professional mentoring, yet hesitate to enter this calling out of low self-esteem, feelings of inadequacy, or a sense of powerlessness. These people are right in line with such figures as Moses, Isaiah, and Jeremiah. For example, when Jeremiah was called by God into service, he prayed, "Ah, Lord God! Truly I do not know how to speak, for I am only a boy."[21]

Gregory offers us encouragement for the journey into mentoring, knowing we are unable to do this work without outside assistance. When we humble ourselves as Moses did, when we allow our lives to be touched as Isaiah did, and when we receive wisdom and truth into our hearts as Jeremiah did, we can step out into the adventure of mentoring, and journey with another across the wilderness of the human soul.

Key to Mentoring

Learn from Isaiah, Jeremiah, and Moses, who overcame their fears and inadequacies, and entered into mentoring with hearts motivated by love.

---

21. Jeremiah 1:6. See also Exodus 3 and Isaiah 6.

CHAPTER 8

Mary Poppins

In the Disney movie *Mary Poppins,* Jane and Michael Banks present to their father a list of qualities describing the perfect nanny. Viewing his children's request as preposterous, Mr. Banks tears up their list and throws it into the fire. When Mary Poppins arrives, she presents the perfect nanny list magically put back together, surprises Mr. Banks with her "cheery disposition" and the children with her no-nonsense approach to discipline.[22]

According to Gregory, the heart of a wise mentor is something like the character of Mary Poppins, requiring both sugar and spice, both praise and correction, both grace and truth. St. Paul offers his own list of qualifications in his first mentoring letter to Timothy: "The saying is sure: whoever aspires to the office of bishop desires a noble task."[23] The Greek word used by Paul for bishop in this sentence, *episkopos,* refers to anyone who oversees the spiritual life of others, not just professional clergy. Paul understands mentoring as a noble task. Among the requirements for carrying out this noble task Paul includes being "above reproach, married only once, temperate, sensible, respectable, hospitable, an apt teacher, not a drunkard, not violent but gentle, not quarrelsome, and not a lover of money."[24] This list recognizes the importance of personal passion, yet warns of self-indulgence. It both encourages and warns mentors, as though Paul is saying, "I celebrate your desire to mentor others, but you must first understand what you are seeking. Fail to examine your motives as you enter into soul care, and you will surely trip and fall in your hurry to be seen by others as a leader."

Like Mary Poppins, a wise mentor shapes the life of the mentee with both sugar and spice, with encouragement and exhortation, with both praise and correction. With a healthy diet of both commendations and admonitions, we can better prepare for the journey ahead. Paul's list includes both positive and negative qualifications for mentors. The positive

22. "The Perfect Nanny" by Richard M. Sherman and Robert B. Sherman, from the 1964 Disney film *Mary Poppins,* see http://www.disneyclips.com/lyrics/lyricsmary3.html (accessed on July 15, 2014).

23. 1 Timothy 3:1.

24. 1 Timothy 3:2–3.

qualities include integrity, fidelity, temperance, self-control, respectability, hospitality, the ability to teach, and generosity. The negative qualifications are in the form of four warnings: not given to drunkenness, not violent, not quarrelsome, and not a lover of money. In other words, live with balance and moderation.

One of the signs of mature mentoring is a life well-balanced between grace and truth, encouragement and exhortation, praise and correction. Too much praise and mentoring becomes sentimentalized, overlooking the hard work of removing masks and getting down to the truth. Too much confrontation and mentoring turns people off or turns them away. Only when people know they are genuinely loved will they freely receive the truth about themselves, even when it is painful. Only when people hear the truth in a loving way will they be set free from their enslavement to self and learn to truly love others.

Key to Mentoring

One of the signs of mature mentoring is a well-balanced life, offering others both grace and truth, encouragement and exhortation, praise and correction.

CHAPTER 9

Storms at Sea

To help us better understand the challenges of mentoring, Gregory invites us out to sea. On a calm day, we may leisurely discuss the ideals of mentoring, looking out on the glassy sea as we relax together in our deck chairs sipping tropical drinks. On his travels by sea across the Mediterranean to Constantinople and back, Gregory faced real storms at sea. He also faced many personal and professional storms as both a civic and spiritual leader.

If you haven't developed the virtue of humility, try going to sea. Stand behind the wheel, and see how easy (or hard) it is to steer the ship. Feel your life filled with gentle breezes of praise, just as the sails fill with gentle westerly winds. As Gregory writes, "an inexperienced sailor can steer a ship in calm waters, but even an experienced seaman is disordered by a storm."[25] Gregory describes our inner life as "the ship of the heart," in which we are "constantly shaken by storms of thoughts, tossed back and forth, until it is shattered . . ."[26] Gregory's phrase "ship of the heart" offers a beautiful metaphor for our spiritual lives, a symbol common in the ancient world for a faith community. Within this symbolism, people of faith are viewed as voyagers on a ship, on which we are carried together across the rough seas of life to the other side.[27] Storms will come, including personal and professional storms, mental and moral storms, physical and financial storms. How will we weather the winds and waves that hit our lives over the years?

Many who enter into soul mentoring will initially think to themselves how easy it is to guide the life of another. They may even think what good work they are doing, helping someone else. Our minds are easily fooled, lulled by the calm before a storm. If you have a difficult time letting go of self-centered ways of thinking on a calm day, it will be even more difficult to learn to walk humbly in high seas. Healthy life disciplines, such as doing acts of kindness for others, are easily practiced in a time of calm, but often are thrown overboard in a storm.

Amongst such dangers as these, what course are we to plot? Clearly, if someone's life has already been tested by storms and they have grown in character, they are better prepared to accept mentorship when the opportunity arises. Those novices who have only sailed calm seas, who lack basic inner virtues such as steadfastness, courage, and humility, should stay away from the wheelhouse. If you have been given a talent, it is wise to put that talent into use, investing your life in the lives of others.[28] Yet there are some who are all too eager to take the helm. Striving for positions of authority, they become an obstacle to others through their immaturity. Every ship needs a doctor on board, but if the doctor is seasick, it's presumptuous to think they will be of any help in healing others.

Sometimes, the only way to break into a selfish person's life is through a storm that hits the ship of the heart. One of the great soul mentors of eighteenth-century England, John Newton (1725–1807), began his seaman's career as a hot-headed, arrogant youth. John first went to sea with his father

25. Gregory, *Pastoral Rule*, 42.
26. Ibid..
27. See Mark 4:35–41, and 1 Peter 3:20–21.
28. Gregory refers in this chapter to Matthew 25:14–30, the parable of the Talents.

at age eleven, in the year 1736. He spent the next decade at sea, aboard merchant ships, navy vessels, and slave ships, as an unruly, self-centered man, full of uncouth behavior. In 1748, at the age of twenty-three, while aboard the merchant ship *Greyhound* bound for Liverpool, Newton had a profound spiritual experience in the midst of a severe storm at sea off the coast of Ireland. Out of fear for his life, Newton cried out to God for help, as the *Greyhound* took on water and threatened to sink. He continued in the seafaring slave trade for another six years. In 1755, at age thirty, he came ashore, took up work as a surveyor in Liverpool, studied biblical languages on the side, and offered his services as a lay preacher. At age thirty-nine, in 1764, Newton was ordained by the Church of England.

During four decades of service in vocational mentoring, Newton wrote over 200 hymns, including the lyrics of one of the world's best-loved hymns, "Amazing Grace." He became well-loved in his local community for his preaching and wise care as a pastor. He also was instrumental in the abolition movement in England, mentoring William Wilberforce. In 1788, thirty-four years after retiring from his work as a slave trader, Newton wrote a short pamphlet, *Thoughts upon the African slave trade,* which was distributed to all the members of Parliament, offering personal insights into the horrors of that trade, assisting the abolitionist cause led by member of Parliament William Wilberforce. Newton lived to see the passage of the Slave Trade Act of 1807, an act abolishing the slave trade in the British Empire. He died that same year, at the age of eighty-two. Millions around the world still sing the lyrics he wrote over 200 years ago:

> Through many dangers, toils, and snares,
> I have already come;
> 'Tis grace has brought me safe thus far,
> And grace will lead me home.[29]

Key to Mentoring

Take time to become a seasoned mentor by being with people in their ship of the heart, in the midst of storms, as they face "many dangers, toils, and snares."

---

29. Verse three of "Amazing Grace" by John Newton, quoted from *Hymns for the Living Church,* 288.

CHAPTER 10

Water for Thirsty Hearts

On our first fifty-mile hike in Olympic National Park in 2003, our family ran out of water on a tough five-mile stretch of trail on a steep ridge with many switchbacks but no water source along the way. Even though huckleberries were plentiful, by the time we reached the lake in the upper valley on that hot August afternoon, our mouths were parched and our bodies drained of energy.

Without water, we perish. We are thirsty creatures and need water to live. Souls are no different. Soul thirst is a primal human condition. Gregory describes a mentor as someone who is "such a student of how to live that [she] is able to water the arid hearts of [her] neighbors with the streams of . . . teaching."[30] Mentoring is watering arid hearts. In Gregory's view, the character of the caregiver is more important than techniques of caregiving.

For anyone wanting to know what to look for in a mentor, Gregory provides excellent guidance. Repeatedly in Part One of *Pastoral Care*, Gregory emphasizes the heart character of a wise mentor. Maturity does not come quickly or easily. Many old ways of life need to be shed. Many new habits and inner disciplines of the heart need to be developed. Essential to grasping Gregory's insight is allowing the streams of love and truth to flow into our own hearts. Prayer and meditation bring us to the source of living water. Unless our inner wells are filled, we will not have water sufficient to help quench the soul thirst of others. What qualities are most needed for the care of souls? If the human heart is a barren wilderness, mentoring is watering thirsty hearts. There are many ways to water arid souls. Below, I've paraphrased Gregory's list of mentoring qualities found at the end of Part One,[31] and I've drawn upon the wisdom of St. Paul from the twelfth chapter of his Letter to the Romans. As you look over this list of mentoring qualities, consider how they are currently developing in your life.

- Live by example, letting your way of life speak more than your many words. "Let love be genuine . . ." (Romans 12:9)

30. Gregory, *Pastoral Rule*, 43–44.
31. See Gregory, *Pastoral Rule*, Part 1, chapter 10.

- Dedicate yourself to excellence and goodness in your way of life. "Love one another with mutual affection; outdo one another in showing honor." (Romans 12:10; Verses below also from Romans 12.)

- Turn away from self-indulgent passions and seek to live a good life. "Hate what is evil, hold fast to what is good." (9)

- Avoid the seductions of worldly prosperity and the intimidations of adversity. "Do not be overcome by evil, but overcome evil with good." (21)

- Treasure riches of the inner life. "Do not lag in zeal, be ardent in spirit . . ." (11)

- Remain steadfast in the face of physical suffering and troubles. "Rejoice in hope, be patient in suffering . . ." (12)

- Weed out greed and plant generosity in the garden of your soul as well as in the lives of others. "Contribute to the needs of the saints; extend hospitality to strangers." (13)

- Be the first to offer the gift of forgiveness and compassion. "If it is possible, so far as it depends on you, live peaceably with all." (18)

- Avoid doing wrong, and take full responsibility for any evil in your life. "Do not repay anyone evil for evil, but take thought for what is noble in the sight of all." (17)

- Be willing to suffer with those who suffer, and celebrate with those who celebrate. "Rejoice with those who rejoice, weep with those who weep." (15)

- Be a lifelong student and a student of life, filling your well with water from the eternal springs of wisdom, able to refresh many others from the abundance within your own soul. "If your enemies are hungry, feed them; if they are thirsty, give them something to drink . . ." (20)

- Live in intimacy with God through daily experiences of meditation and prayer. "Persevere in prayer." (12)

Mentoring Inventory: Part One

As we come to the end of Part One of *Soul Mentoring*, I invite you to take a few moments to review the opening ten chapters of Gregory's mentoring guidebook and reflect on your own life experience. Consider ways you may deepen your experience of mentoring or help you find a wise mentor by implementing Gregory's wisdom. Below is a checklist, a mentoring inventory, drawn from Part One, chapter 11 of *Pastoral Care*. In each statement below, assess your experience of mentoring, either as a giver or receiver, and write in the left margin next to each statement with the number that most describes where you are at this time.

3 – strongly agree and mostly true of me

2 – somewhat agree and partially true of me

1 – somewhat disagree and mostly not true of me

- I regularly evaluate my life, examining it for struggles, vices, failures, and difficulties.

- I often take time to meditate and to pray for someone's spiritual growth.

- I am willing to learn how to pray and meditate.

- I try to improve my own way of life by allowing divine light and truth to shine upon my path, as I seek to walk in the light.

- I seek to help people who are inwardly disabled, unable to walk in the good and loving way of life, aware that they often know the good way, but due to struggles in their heart, fail to live the life they long for.

- I desire to "lift . . . drooping hands and strengthen . . . weak knees, and make straight paths for . . . feet, so that what is lame may not be put out of joint, but rather be healed."[32]

- I am developing my nose for discernment, and I can discern the difference between the sweet fragrance of virtue and the bad odor of corruption within others.

- I avoid playing the busybody or private investigator in someone's life, knowing discernment does not come from stirring up the pond or jumping too quickly to judgment, but rather from inner clarity that comes from quiet attentiveness.

- I acknowledge my own brokenness and my inability to walk in the way of wisdom and love. Sometimes, I am bowed down with the weight of life's cares and forget to look up to the lofty ideals and eternal wisdom from above. My life is sometimes choked off by anxieties and cares, as

---

32. Hebrews 12:12–13.

well as by the riches, and pleasures of life, and thus I do not bear as much fruit as I could.[33]

- My vision of others is often blurry, my eyes are often weary, and I often become blinded by self-centeredness. I often have a hard time helping others clearly see how best to live and love. When I admit my blindness, turn to the light, and apply wisdom to situations I face, then I begin once again to see clearly and better know how to care for others.[34]

- I do my best to weed out greed from my soul. I intentionally plant gratitude in my inner garden, even when I don't feel thankful.

- I regularly unburden my life of any unhealthy loads I've been carrying, sharing them with a wise mentor who can care for my soul and help bear my burdens. I realize that I am unable to help cleanse the soul of another when I am weighed down by my own spiritual troubles and burdens. I seek to live out Paul's instruction to "carry each other's burdens, and in this way . . . fulfill the law of Christ."[35]

After taking this inventory, tally up your points. If you scored 24–36, you serve well as a mentor for others. If you scored 12–24, you are developing many excellent traits for mentoring and still have plenty of room for growth. If you scored below 12, you are just beginning your journey into soul care and would benefit from having a mentor to help you enter this way of life.

33. See Psalm 37:7 and Luke 8:14, two verses quoted by Gregory in Part One, chapter 11.

34. See Revelation 3:18 and Ephesians 5:8–14.

35. Galatians 6:2.

Part Two

The Character of a Mentor—Drinking from Mountain Streams

D uring the summer of 2013, my wife and I, along with our son and his girlfriend, hiked a sixty-mile loop in Yosemite National Park, which included several days of trekking along the Merced River. In the middle of the week, while twenty-five miles from our car, we hiked overland about seven miles, from the base of Red Peak to Washburn Lake, down the Red Peak Fork valley, over giant slabs of granite puzzle pieces, through cool forests, along glacier-smoothed stone, down to the Merced River. The last half mile down this valley was a steep descent, and we slowly found our own switchback pathway down the broken granite face. When we arrived at the edge of the Merced, we were hot, sweaty, hungry, and ready for a lunch break. Taking off our backpacks, boots, and socks, we filled our water bottles from the cool waters of the Merced and drank deeply. *Merced* is the Spanish word for mercy or favor. That day, in the heat of noonday sun in the high country, drinking from a mountain stream was truly a gift of mercy.

In the opening section of Part Two of *Pastoral Care*, Gregory describes the character of a spiritual mentor as an exemplary way of living, one that "transcends that of the people."[1] The example he provides is from rural life, that of a shepherd caring for a flock of sheep in a wilderness.

---

1. Gregory, *Pastoral Rule*, 49.

In the best-known of all the Psalms, the Twenty-Third Psalm, God is described as a shepherd. With the help of our shepherd, we are guided to mountain streams and green pastures, restored, led along the path of life, protected from evil, provided for in abundance, and continuously surrounded with goodness and love.

In the opening chapter of Part Two, Gregory offers readers a top ten list of mentoring qualities to help guide us in caring for others. These ten qualities outline Gregory's design for development of mentors and mentees. As you review the next section, consider where your life stands in relation to each of these ten qualities, and how such ways of life may improve the way you mentor others, or the way others are mentoring you. Here are Gregory's top ten qualities of soul mentors:

- Integrity

- Walking the talk

- Wisdom in silence and speech

- Compassion and contemplation

- Mothering and fathering

- Inside-out and outside-in

- Motivated by the love of God

- Discernment of vice and virtue

- Mercy triumphs over judgment

- Meditation upon divine wisdom.

With Gregory as our guide, we will explore each of these qualities in detail as a step-by-step guide for mentoring others, as well as a helpful summary of what to look for when being mentored by another.

CHAPTER 11

Integrity

A mentor is called to a life of integrity, not merely washing the body, but seeking to keep even the mind and heart clean. Just as dirty hands can make us sick physically, impure thoughts can pollute a person inwardly. Mentors learn first to wash their own life before they wash the lives of others: otherwise, whatever they touch will be soiled with unhealthy ideas and motives. As the wise sage declared centuries ago, "purify yourselves, you who carry vessels of the Lord."[2] Everyone who mentors others carries sacred vessels. People are like clay jars containing sacred treasures. We are wise to clean our hearts and minds before we seek to help someone else clean their soul vessel. We are easily puffed up with self-importance or deflated by lust and greed. Such forces wreak havoc upon the soul of a mentor. If neglected, such temptations and vices will bring us down.

"Create in me a clean heart, O God."[3] This prayer for purity was first written thirty centuries ago by a man who had so deeply dirtied his heart he feared being abandoned by God forever. God invites us all to bring out into the open impurities within our lives that we are powerless to cleanse, and to seek God's cleansing mercy. Ancient prayers speak across centuries, calling us back into a life of integrity and wholeness.

Our culture often presents a message of self-empowerment and overcoming impurities and inner troubles with positive thinking. Unfortunately, we are not like self-cleaning ovens. We don't have a self-cleaning button we can push and, like technological magic, be clean inside. Most humans struggle with inner impurities, in thought, word, and deed. Everyone also has inner struggles with ongoing habits we know are unhealthy and unwholesome. Consider the sign displayed at public pools: "Please shower before entering pool." Soul mentors seek to live with as much integrity as possible as we step into lives of others.

Gregory writes visually. In the opening chapter of Part Two, he describes people as sacred vessels. I own a pottery wheel and have some

2. Isaiah 52:11.
3. Psalm 51:10.

27

experience throwing clay pots. My potter friends make throwing clay look easy; it is not. Your hands and arms are caked with clay. Your apron, pants, floors, and walls get spattered with the wet clay slip. If you are successful in throwing a clay pot, you still have to trim it, fire it, glaze it, and fire it again. But when you finally open the kiln and pull out your cooled, finished work, you have a beautiful piece of handmade pottery ready for use.

We too are being crafted into vessels for use. God loves a hands-on approach to this labor of love. With hands of truth and grace surrounding our lives, God centers us, opens us, and shapes us into sacred vessels to be used by God in the lives of others. Gregory's vision of soul care offers practical guidance and a deep sense of hope. For this work is not primarily ours—unseen hands are upon us, cleansing, centering, opening, shaping, firing, filling, using. We are being shaped and filled to pour out our lives into others, bringing soul refreshment.

Throughout his book on *Pastoral Care*, Gregory gives quiet tribute to his mentor Benedict, drawing upon principles and wisdom from *The Rule of St. Benedict*. Benedict instructed his community regarding living with integrity:

> We urge the entire community . . . to keep its manner of life most pure and to wash away . . . the negligences of other times. This we can do in a fitting manner by refusing to indulge evil habits and by devoting ourselves to prayer with tears, to reading, to compunction of heart and self-denial.[4]

If our lives are disturbed or discolored by the stain of soul impurities, we are wise to seek the gift of divine grace to cleanse our life through forgiveness, "to wash away the negligences," and to purify our mind and heart through prayers, readings, and acts of spiritual renewal. Only then can we truly "carry the sacred vessels"—the lives of others—into the beautiful sacred space of the heart.

Key to Mentoring

Become aware of the unseen hands are upon our lives, cleansing, centering, opening, shaping, firing, filling, and using us to bring refreshment to others.

4. Benedict, *The Rule of St. Benedict*, 71, RB 49:2–4. All quotations from *The Rule of St. Benedict* are from Timothy Fry, ed., *RB 1980: The Rule of St. Benedict in English*, listed in the notes as RB with chapter and verse.

CHAPTER 12

Walking the Talk

Having spent many summers with my family backpacking in mountainous national parks, I feel a connection in my muscles and bones with Gregory's picture of ascending high places as a pattern for soul care. During our family hikes, we have often climbed to the highest ridge or peak in an area, surveying the landscape from the mountaintop, gaining new perspectives on life once we return to the valleys, lakes, and meadows below.

Drawing upon an ancient metaphor for faith, that of walking along a path, Gregory calls mentors to "walk the talk," calling all who enter into soul care to match our words with our lives. Reading trail guides is one way to experience the wonder and beauty of the high country of such a place as Glacier National Park. I study such trail guides for months before stepping out from a trailhead. When looking for a reliable trail guidebook, I look for an authorwho has personally walked those trails, and thus writes from personal experience hiking and climbing in the high country, not just theoretical knowledge of those paths and places.

Mentors lead by example, so that their way of life might show others a good way to live. Those who speak of the highest principles are wise to live out those lofty ideals in the lowest places of daily life. What we say will enter the hearts of hearers more fully when the way we live reflects the way we speak, our words fully supported by our lives. As the prophet cried out centuries ago, "Get you up to a high mountain . . . lift up your voice with strength . . ."[5] Any who dare to declare good tidings through lofty words must leave behind the lower ways of the world, and strive to climb above corrupt paths in their way of living as well as in their way of speaking. We can guide others to the high places more easily when we have previously walked that higher path in our own life.

In the same way, we who dare to mentor another must strive to walk along the paths to the heights of faith, hope, and love, struggling and stumbling along the way to be sure, yet pressing on to attain the summits of maturity. As Benedict wrote regarding leading others by example: "Point out to

---

5. Isaiah 40:9.

them all that is good . . . more by example than by words . . . demonstrating God's instructions . . . by a living example."[6] Only when we have worn out several pairs of hiking boots will we begin to truly gain perspective on the terrain and trail wisdom involved in guiding others to great heights, with our words flowing from the integrity of our hearts like cascading streams that flow into the valleys from mountain heights.

Key to Mentoring

Strive to walk the talk, intentionally living according to the truths you speak, walking spiritual paths to the heights of faith, hope, and love, pressing on to attain the summits of maturity.

CHAPTER 13

Wisdom in Silence and Speech

An ancient Jewish proverb reads, "Salt is good; but if salt has lost its saltiness, how can you season it? Have salt in yourselves, and be at peace with one another."[7] Words are like salt. Mentors are salty people with their words. We choose words sparingly, but sprinkle vigorously when necessary. Some dishes need more salt. Likewise, some people need the preserving and correcting salt of truth sprinkled liberally upon their lives. Fail to do this, and we allow people to decay like raw meat in the sun.

Mentors need to be discerning in our silence and salty in our words. Too much silence and we hold back wise words that need to be said; but too many words and we say what should not be said. Both silence and speech can lead to error. Indiscreet mentors talk too much, often out of insecurity in silence, and thus fail to attend to the needs of the people they are mentoring. Timid mentors are silent, too often out of fear of doing something wrong, and thus fail to assist in correcting faults when they are discovered. A word of correction can be like a key that opens hidden doors into the

6. RB 2:12.
7. Mark 9:50.

soul. Therefore, use a little salt in your speech with people, for as the ancient proverb asserts, "Salt is good."

We are wise to keep guard over our lips, even avoiding saying the right words too often, for what is said can easily be overlooked or lost when it is spoken in haste or without care. When looking for a wise mentor, seek someone who uses words wisely, and who knows the value of silence. As Solomon said in ancient times,

> Guard your steps when you go to the house of God; to draw near to listen is better than the sacrifice offered by fools; for they do not know how to keep from doing evil. Never be rash with your mouth, nor let your heart be quick to utter a word before God, for God is in heaven, and you upon earth; therefore let your words be few.[8]

The second half of the ancient Jewish proverb Gregory cites invites salty people to live at peace with others. "Have salt in yourselves, and be at peace with one another." The right amount of salt in our lives is healthy. With the right amount of salt in our words, we live at peace with one another. Too many words, like too much salt, ruins the meal. Failing to practice silence allows noise and excess words to bring discord into our lives like a pack of yelping dogs. One of the sure marks of a wise mentor is someone well-seasoned and balanced in the practice of silence and speech. Echoing *The Rule of St Benedict*, Gregory holds silence in high esteem, especially in mentoring. As Benedict wrote,

> Indeed, so important is silence that permission to speak should seldom be granted even to mature disciples, no matter how good or holy or constructive their talk, because it is written: 'In a flood of words you will not avoid sin (Prov 10:19)'; and elsewhere, 'The tongue holds the key to life and death (Prov 18:21).' Speaking and teaching are the master's task; the disciple is to be silent and listen."[9]

Every person is given a different measure of faith to shake out upon this world. Better to think before opening our mouths and pouring out a torrent of salty speech. We might as well open our mouths every now and then and insert a shoe before we trouble others with our hasty and unwise flurry of words.

8. Ecclesiastes 5:1–2.
9. RB 6:3–6.

Key to Mentoring

One of the sure marks of a wise mentor is someone well-seasoned and balanced in the practices of silence and speech.

CHAPTER 14

Compassion and Contemplation

In the summer of 2011, our family hiked to the 13,310' summit of Mount Alice in Rocky Mountain National Park. From that sunny vantage point, we feasted our eyes north and south along the Continental Divide, the tallest spine in North America. We looked down into the beautiful mountain valley between Mount Alice and Longs Peak, a meadowland filled with small lakes including Snowbank Lake, Lion lakes, and Castle Lake. We also looked down on Thunder Lake thousands of feet below us sparkling in the afternoon sun. Later that evening, we stood at the shore of Thunder Lake near our campsite, looking back up at the golden peak of Mount Alice, with a sense of wonder that just a few hours earlier we were standing upon those heights. I've always loved the new perspective that comes from hiking in the backcountry of a national park. Once we get a few miles away from the trailhead, out into the wildness, our eyes and souls are filled with a renewed sense of wonder at the beauty and quiet of nature away from the distractions and noise of civilization.

Contemplation is like looking from a mountain top into a valley where you normally live. From that height, the whole valley takes on a new perspective. Little stuff doesn't seem quite so important. Petty squabbles and irritations lose their grip from the heights of contemplation, where we can survey the glory of the landscape around us. Whether it is simply the thin air or the late afternoon sun glinting in our eyes, from atop the mountain the world seems filled with wonder and beauty. Heading up the mountain is truly a labor, every step taken with intention and exertion. Coming back down, after contemplative time on the mountain top, our feet seem lighter and filled with new life. The whole mountainside seems eager to move downward into the valleys below, with little brooklets singing their simple melodies of joy as they cascade over stones, around clumps of wildflowers bowing with delight in the late afternoon wind. From the heights of contemplation, the soul moves joyfully into the valleys below with compassion, where we pour ourselves out on behalf of people in their low places.

A soul mentor is someone who is willing to walk in the valleys because they have journeyed to the heights, someone moved with compassion because they have been seasoned with contemplation. A mentor welcomes the burdens of others, willing to descend into the deep places of human suffering out of the depths of love. A mentor also ascends with those burdens, through paths of meditation and contemplation, lifting others beyond narrow horizons into the radiant visions on the heights.

Those who only pursue lofty things often neglect the needs of neighbors. Those who only bear the burdens of neighbors often neglect the pursuit of paradise. Saints guide us along this sacred way: up into unspeakable wonders of light through contemplation, and down into darkness to attend to the lowly needs of the weak.[10]

Consider Jacob and Moses, who both stood face-to-face with God. Jacob beheld angels ascending and descending the ladder of heaven, showing us the importance of both ascending in contemplation and descending in compassion. In the same way, Moses went up the mountain to be in the presence of God, in order to better attend to the needs and burdens of the people in the valley below. Whenever Moses was uncertain how to deal with a person's problem, he went back up the mountain before the presence of God.

When we are unsure how to best care for the life of another, we are wise to return to the inward journey, to go back up the sacred mountain to renew our vision. The life of Jesus of Nazareth shows us the same pattern. He spent time on the mountaintop in intimacy with God to be spiritually renewed before going back down into the valley to live among people in the ordinary places. A mentor's path keeps calling us higher through times of contemplation. There, upon the heights of love, we begin to see the mist clear away. There we are renewed, that we might walk in love among the depths of human suffering. Contemplation finds her highest delight when moved with compassion to the lowest places in people's lives.

Gregory spent joyful portions of his life within the cloister, devoting his days to quiet contemplation from the heights of spiritual ascent into the presence of God. Gregory recalled the examples of Moses and Jesus, who

10. Gregory refers to 2 Corinthians 12:2–3 and 1 Corinthians 7:2, 5 in this passage.

both went up to mountain heights to encounter God, and went down to the valleys to bring compassion to the people. As in Jacob's vision of angels ascending and descending, Gregory invites us to ascend and descend, living a well-balanced life of contemplation and compassion. We ascend to the heights of contemplation in order to joyfully cascade into the valley to serve others with compassion.

Like hiking up a mountain, there are no shortcuts into the practice of contemplation. Every time I've hiked along switchbacks up a steep mountainside, I've been tempted to cut corners and shorten the journey. But such shortcuts only increase the difficulties and dangers of the journey. Step by faithful step, as we intentionally move away from our busy lives and step out upon the contemplative way, we begin to discover a new rhythm, a new way of seeing, a new way of living. Here are five ways to begin to practice the ancient art of contemplation.

First, sit still and breathe. Take a few minutes in the morning to sit in the same place, perhaps in a comfortable chair by a window. Just sit. Try not to fidget. Step away from doing and enjoy time for being. Be still. Quiet your body. Quiet your mind. Quiet your soul. Take ten slow, deep breaths, and exhale them slowly, feeling your body fill with breath, then empty of breath. Relax your body as you breathe in and out.

Second, be aware. Feel the touch of your feet on the floor, your legs touching the chair, the weight of your body resting on your seat, your back touching the back of the chair, your shoulder muscles, neck, lips, nose, eyes, ears, and scalp. Become aware of the air around you. Smell, see, feel, hear, and taste the world around you and within you at this moment.

Third, focus. Center your attention upon a single focal point. Try lighting a candle and focusing your attention on the flame. Some focus their mind and heart on a sacred word or phrase, breathing a short prayer, inhaling and exhaling the word or phrase. Others play quiet music to help focus the soul. Gently turn away from any distraction that comes along (whether physical or mental), and return to your focal point. Or select a beautiful tree, a nature photo, or a work of art to center your attention on. In his best-selling book *The Nature Principle*, Richard Louv writes of the power of focusing upon the natural world to find renewal:

> My eyes settled on a single cottonwood at the river, its branches and upper leaves waving in a slow rhythm above all the others. An hour, perhaps more, went by. Tension crawled up and out of me. It seemed to twist in the air above the green field. Then it was

gone. And something better took its place. Twenty-four years later, I often think about that cottonwood at the river's edge, and similar moments of inexplicable wonder, times when I received from nature just what I needed: an elusive *it* for which I have no name. [11]

Fourth, relax. Pace yourself. Try not to get impatient. Begin with small steps and take them slowly. Try not to be in a hurry. Laugh a lot. Raise your shoulders up to your cheeks, count to ten, then drop them to relax the muscles around your neck. Squeeze up your face into a tight contortion as you breathe in a long inhale, then let all the muscles in your face and body relax as you breathe out a long sigh of relief.

Fifth, drink deeply of God's presence. Like a deer at a stream, stoop low and drink deeply. Fill your soul with God's goodness and love. God is the highest goal of our contemplation. Our lives come from God and go to God. Why not go now to the source of refreshment and renewal? Once filled, go and pour your life out in compassion to help others who are thirsty.

Key to Mentoring

Seek to live a well-balanced life of contemplation and compassion, both ascending to the heights of contemplation and descending into the valley of compassionate service.

CHAPTER 15

Mothering and Fathering

My favorite Vincent van Gogh painting is titled "First Steps." In the scene, a baby girl dressed in pink is taking her first steps. The mother has just set the one-year-old child down in the backyard vegetable garden of a simple cottage. The father kneels in the foreground with outstretched arms to receive his daughter. A child's first steps are one of the sweetest moments in the life

11. Louv, *The Nature Principle*, 2.

of a father and mother. As a baby stands up and steps forward for the first time, she seeks an inner balance—left foot, right foot, left, right.

A soul mentor, regardless of their gender, learns to skillfully balance the gentle discipline of a father and the disciplined gentleness of a mother. As Gregory writes, "Either discipline or kindness is lacking if one is ever exercised independently of the other."[12] Remember the parable of the Good Samaritan. The Samaritan applied both wine and oil to the stranger's wounds as an act of loving his neighbor.[13] In seeking to heal inner wounds of the soul, use both strictness and gentleness. As the beloved ancient poem instructs us, "Your rod and your staff—they comfort me."[14] With the rod, we are corrected and trained. With the staff, we are supported and restored. Do not allow your love to grow soft, and do not let your discipline exasperate. Wise mentors keep their spiritual zeal in control, and let their kindness overflow—but not more than is appropriate. St. Peter instructed mentors to serve eagerly, telling us, "Do not lord it over those in your charge, but be examples to the flock."[15] The art of mentoring unites justice and mercy in the fire of the soul, inspiring both respect and wonder in those under our care.

Gregory understood mentoring in terms of balance. Soul care seeks to balance grace and truth, mercy and justice, gentleness and discipline. On one hand, we correct, exhort, and train others, seeking to do so with love. On the other hand, we nurture, comfort, and care for others, seeking to do so with truth. Mentors learn the inner skill of balancing opposing forces, holding them together in the fire of the soul, and forging them into discernment tools to bring about healing of inner wounds and growth of the soul.

Gregory compares this balance to the influence of a mother and a father upon a child, keeping in mind the kindness of a mother and the discipline of a father. Of course, these are stereotypes of parenting, yet they are worthy of consideration when seeking to influence the growth of another person. Either side of the careful balance of leniency or legalism tends to stifle growth in a family. In the same way, the ancient art of soul mentoring holds mercy and justice in balance for the sake of inner growth in others. Gregory draws once again upon the teachings of Benedict, who wrote about the role of a mentor in a monastery:

12. Gregory, *Pastoral Rule*, 67. Cf. Gregory, *Morals on the Book of Job*, 20.5.14.

13. See Luke 10:25–37.

14. Psalm 23:4.

15. 1 Peter 5:2–3.

He must be chaste, temperate and merciful. He should always *let mercy triumph over judgment* so that he too may win mercy. He must hate faults but love the brothers. When he must [discipline] them, he should use prudence and avoid extremes; otherwise, by rubbing too hard to remove the rust, he may break the vessel. He is to distrust his own frailty and remember *not to crush the bruised reed.* By this we do not mean that he should allow faults to flourish, but rather, as we have already said, he should prune them away with prudence and love as he sees best for each individual.[16]

Key to Mentoring

Mentors learn the inner skill of balancing gentleness and discipline, holding them together in the fire of the soul, and forging them into discernment tools to bring inner growth.

CHAPTER 16

Inside-Out and Outside-In

Most of us learned in kindergarten what is needed for a seed to grow. Both external and internal forces work upon and within the seed to bring about germination. Without the external elements of oxygen, temperature, and water the seed will never sprout. Likewise, without the awakening inner elements hidden within the embryo of the seed, germination will also never take place.

Excellent mentoring pays attention to both the inside and the outside of life. Two opposite problems are common among people: either we neglect our internal lives by focusing too much attention upon external demands; or we neglect external responsibilities by being too preoccupied with our interior lives. Too much anxiety over external demands and we impoverish our inner life; too much focus on the inner life and we neglect the needs of our neighbor.

16. RB 64:9–14. Italics are original and quotes from James 2:13 and Isaiah 42:3.

Some mentors eagerly volunteer for any external opportunity that comes up. They seem to find their life's purpose in exhausting themselves with activity. When they are finally able to spend a few minutes in quiet, they have forgotten how to find rest for their soul. While enjoying their busy external life, such mentors become inwardly shallow and thus have little to give others. Those who have a desire to grow spiritually stumble over the poor example offered by the very mentors who were supposed to be caring for their soul.

On the other side of the problem, there are those who focus all their attention upon their inner life but neglect of the needs of the others around them. The result is that people are less likely to listen to their guidance, for they fail to take seriously the issues of this present life. Good teaching fails to enter the soil of the mind when sown with disregard for others or lack of compassion.

The seed of wisdom grows best when a mentor plants with love and waters the heart with kindness. For this reason, we need to find ways to provide for both the physical and spiritual needs of people. We must attend to outer concerns of daily life as needed, but keep watch over the inner life as well—both our own inner lives and the inner lives of those in our care.

Personal growth takes place when attention is given to both the exterior and interior lives of others. According to Gregory, wise mentors keep their lives balanced, and are attentive to both physical and spiritual needs. As in Gregory's day, so in our time this balance can be difficult to maintain. Exterior forces demand much of our attention, leaving little time or energy for renewing our interior lives. When we finally come into a time of quiet, we are often so distracted, weary, or restless that we find it hard to settle down to care for our own souls. It can seem like too much work to pray, mediate, journal, wait attentively, listen, or simply sit in silence. How much easier it is to fill such times with television shows, magazines, computers or other electronic devices, phone calls, or other distractions. When we neglect our own inner lives, we will find that we are less able to care for the inner lives of others, simply because we are too busy, distracted, or weary.

Learning to say no to external demands is an ancient tool of soul care. Learning to cease speaking and begin listening is also an ancient way of soul mentoring. How easy is it for you to ignore the ringing of your cell phone or turn off the television? How often do you interrupt a conversation with a person to attend to some electronic distraction? How many minutes each day to you devote to the care of the soul, both your own and those of others? What does this say about how you are balancing inner and outer life at this time?

Gregory encourages "moderate vigilance of the heart," aware of some who go overboard, neglecting outside realities around them. Spiritual disciplines have a vital role in personal growth, but they may also be used in unhealthy ways, causing harm to the soul as well as harm to relationships. For example, those who practice fasting may feel superior to others who overeat or disdain those who enjoy a good meal. I knew a man who meditated in his closet day and night, seldom helping around the house or spending quality time with his spouse. Out of neglect for his wife, he harmed his marriage through excessive practice of his spiritual life. As humans we are hybrids, sharing physical and spiritual lives within the same skin. Overload either realm and we bring harm to ourselves and to others.

There are also some who practice spirituality for the sake of impressing others. Jesus warns against showing off our spirituality in order to impress others. Better to "go into your room and shut the door and pray . . . in secret; and [God] who sees in secret will reward you."[17] Once you've finished with your time of quiet meditation or prayer, go and fold the laundry or weed the garden. Like a garden, we too are designed to grow, from the inside out and from the outside in. We are wise to attend with love to both the outer and inner lives of those in our care. The seed of wisdom germinates in the human heart when planted with compassion and watered with kindness.

Key to Mentoring

Wise mentors keep life in balance, attentive to life from the outside in and from the inside out, in our own lives as well as in the lives of others.

17. Matthew 6:6.

CHAPTER 17

Motivated by Love and Truth

Gregory writes with a moderate voice, holding up the scales of love and truth, weighing out these forces for the most good in and for others. He uses a beautiful phrase, telling us that it is necessary that soul mentoring "be tempered by the great art of moderation."[18] Gregory learned this "great art of moderation" from his mentor, Benedict, who is known for his voice of moderation. As Benedict wrote in his prologue,

> Therefore, we intend to establish a school for the Lord's service. In drawing up its regulations, we hope to set down nothing harsh, nothing burdensome. The good of all concerned however, may prompt us to a little strictness in order to amend faults and to safeguard love. Do not be daunted immediately by fear and run away from the road that leads to salvation.[19]

The practice of the "great art of moderation" tempers truth with love and seasons love with truth. Both love and truth flow from the high country into our lives, poured out through the art of mentoring. I appreciate Gregory's voice of moderation, encouraging mentors to listen and learn from their mentees, just as Peter was corrected by Paul, and David confronted by the Prophet Nathan. Together, we seek that ancient balance between love and truth.

While caring for others, mentors make it a high priority to be watchful over their own lives, lest they become motivated more by a desire to please others than by love and truth. The desire to be loved by others can lead a mentor to overlook the faults of others simply because we are afraid they will reject us if we correct them. Mentors seek to hold mentees accountable; but sometimes, out of self-love, they also seek to flatter others to win their approval.

There are also some mentors who get caught up the pursuit of self-love and the desire for human praise, elevating themselves above others and playing judge of people's lives. There is a danger of becoming overly

18. Gregory, *Pastoral Rule*, 76.
19. RB Prologue:45–48.

harsh in dealing with someone's weaknesses, rather than offering the gentle touch of correction. Better to desire truth and be motivated by love. Think of Peter, who accepted correction from Paul, or King David, who humbled himself before a prophet's rebuke.[20] The ancient practice of mentoring is tempered by the great art of moderation, so that mentors and mentees may seek truth as well as experience love.

Good mentors seek to lead others by the sweetness of their own lives. Affection is the manner in which we walk, leading both mentors and mentees into the higher realms of love. Those who know they are loved are more eager to listen. As St. Paul wrote, "I try to please everyone in everything I do, not seeking my own advantage, but that of many, so that they may be saved."[21] Those who mentor and those who are mentored are to study the ancient way of love and truth to best know how to be pleasing to others in everything we do.

Gregory once more lives out his name, calling mentors into a life of watchfulness, watching over the lives of others. This vigilance challenges mentors to ask themselves hard questions: Am I out of balance? Am I seeking more to please people or be genuine and truthful? Am I being too harsh with this person, or too lenient? Am I willing to carry the same expectations that I've placed upon the lives of those under my care? How hypocritical am I in my words and in my way of life? Who is holding me accountable and helping me to live with greater integrity at this time? Am I puffed up with knowledge and a sense of self-importance, or am I building others up in love? Again, we hear Paul declare, "We know that 'all of us possess knowledge.' Knowledge puffs up, but love builds up."[22]

What motivates us inwardly to do what we do in soul care? Gregory tells us the only motivation that truly leads to lasting healing and growth is love. He tells us this love is to be expressed person-to-person, with a deep love for the truth, for when we love the truth, the truth sets us free to begin to truly love others. As Jesus teaches, "You will know the truth, and the truth will set you free."[23]

20. Galatians 2:11 and 2 Samuel 12:7.
21. 1 Corinthians 10:33.
22. 1 Corinthians 8:1.
23. John 8:32.

Key to Mentoring

Practice the "great art of moderation," tempering truth with love and seasoning love with truth, so that mentors and mentees alike may know truth and experience love.

CHAPTER 18

Discernment

Children love dressing up for Halloween, putting on costumes and masks then heading out to trick or treat. In our little beach village, children go from shop to shop collecting candy on Halloween afternoon. Our downtown fills with pirates, goblins, princesses, and fairies. In the evening, all these strange masked creatures gather at the elementary school along with their parents and other townsfolk for a Halloween festival, complete with caramel apples, cakewalks, and carnival games. Then the first day of November comes; kids wake up and head off to school wearing no costumes or masks, instead getting back to the good work of education.

As adults, we still love to wear masks. According to Gregory, we often wear virtuous masks to hide our vices, covering our weaknesses with masks of strength, hoping others will not look behind the surface of our lives. I love the line from *The Wizard of Oz*, "Pay no attention to the man behind the green curtain." In the midst of the booming voice of authority and the billowing flames of power, there he is, the bumbling country doctor from Kansas, pretending to be the great and awesome Wizard of Oz. Toto knows better, pulling back the green curtain to reveal the truth. Part of the hard work of mentoring is pulling off masks and pulling back green curtains.

Sometimes vices masquerade as virtues. A stingy person may try to tell you he is frugal, or a wasteful person may pretend she is being generous. Laziness can be rationalized as compassion, while uncontrolled anger is sometimes passed off as zeal. Rash judgment can parade as prompt responsibility, or tardiness as wise deliberation.

What is needed is a watchful heart to see behind outward appearances to inner truth, and thus help a mentee know the difference between vice and virtue. A wise mentor helps a mentee learn to discern. In this way, vices can be kept in check and virtues allowed to grow. Wise mentors do not overlook vices such as greed or wastefulness, laziness or wrath, rashness or tardiness, all of which bring harm. A wise mentor encourages a mentee to develop virtues such as simplicity and generosity, compassion and zeal, responsibility and wisdom.

Mentoring welcomes the wisdom of those who draw back the green curtain. Mentoring involves the boldness to ask for permission to remove a mask and the discernment to understand what lies beneath. This is best done when mutual respect and trust has been established between a mentor and mentee. Without trust, according to Gregory, a mentee may "sin more grievously" by becoming more entrenched in their vices, not allowing virtue to come into the soul. With discernment and mutual respect, masks may be gently removed, and we may begin to allow our souls to be dressed in such authentic virtues as simplicity, generosity, compassion, zeal, responsibility, and wisdom.

Key to Mentoring

Mentoring involves the boldness needed to remove masks and pull back green curtains, and the discernment to understand what lies behind them.

CHAPTER 19

Checkup

Every person struggles with some form of soul trouble. Nobody has it all together. We are all vulnerable to temptation, indiscretion, brokenness, isolation, weakness, corruption, and failure. How we face such hindrances to spiritual growth depends upon how open we are to receiving help, including help from God, as well as the help of a wise mentor. Anyone who has come face-to-face with their own shortcomings knows what a gift it is to receive mercy instead of judgment, acceptance instead of rejection, and grace instead of condemnation. As we allow ourselves to come under scrutiny at a checkup by coming under the care of a mentor, we discover healing in our mind and heart, as well as in relationships with those around us.

Sometimes, a mentor is wise to overlook a person's weaknesses, offering encouragement rather than exhortation. On other occasions though, a mentor needs to bring vices out into the light and carefully examine what is being hidden with them. Much of this depends upon the mentee and how they respond to a mentor's attempts to help them amend their life.

As every medical doctor knows, surgery is not always the best course of treatment, for some people are not strong enough to survive its rigors. Likewise, not every medicine is suitable for every person. Wise mentors, acting as physicians of the soul, check up on the health of a mentee, diagnosing the trouble and helping them seek the best course of treatment for specific ills and ailments. Certain diseases of the soul require careful examination and discernment to bring them out into the light, where healing can begin.

As long as we live in these mortal bodies, we are vulnerable to the weakness of our mortality. Mentors help others learn from their weaknesses, and seek to show mercy to those they are mentoring, especially in the places of their greatest weakness. We are to "bear one another's burdens," being willing to help another person in the places of their greatest weaknesses. Paul calls us to "bear one another's burden, and in this way you will fulfill the law of Christ," which is the law of love.[24] In so doing, we are wise to remember our own shortcomings and seek to restore people with gentleness.

Like a wise physician, Gregory offers options when facing various forms of inner pathology or damage. Many forms of soul sickness lie out of view, well hidden—sometimes, they are even hidden from the soul-sick person themselves. A wise mentee goes in for a regular checkup, willing to have their lives examined by a mentor. A wise mentor, like an experienced medical specialist, seeks to discern the core problem and potential avenues toward health. Sometimes, this requires overlooking faults and offering encouragement and support. Other times, though, a mentor needs to bring out into the open the hidden vices of the heart, helping a mentee see what they are avoiding, ignoring, denying, or repressing. Only through loving accountability, as troubles are brought out into the light of love, can healing truly begin.

24. Galatians 6:2.

Key to Mentoring

A wise mentee goes in for a regular checkup, willing to have their lives examined by a mentor. A wise mentor, like an experienced doctor, seeks to discern the core problem and potential avenues toward health.

CHAPTER 20

Drinking from Mountain Streams

We carry mountain streams with us as we backpack in national parks. I usually carry two water bottles, one liter each, tucked into side pouches of my backpack, easily accessible while hiking further up and farther into places of wild beauty. We hike with a lightweight water pump that filters the water from streams and lakes into our water bottles. Filling all the water bottles requires about fifteen minutes of work, sitting quietly beside a mountain lake or stream. I love this "water time." Whenever water bottles are empty and the need arises, I jump at the opportunity to go get water, knowing the water will refresh my family for the journey ahead, as I am refreshed by sitting still by a mountain lake.

Like carrying water bottles, we are wise to carry soul refreshment with us through the ancient spiritual discipline of *lectio divina,* or sacred meditation upon Scripture. Well-seasoned mentors return to mountain streams to refill their water reserves with the clear water of Scripture. As the psalmist sings to God, "you give them drink from the river of your delights. For with you is the fountain of life . . ."[25]

Gregory calls us to meditate deeply upon ancient wisdom from Scripture, refreshing our souls daily. The wisdom of the sacred Word will restore us, mature our lives, and provide clarity to help us walk alongside others who are hurting. Our hearts shrivel when we fill our lives with human distractions, causing us to waste away as though we lived among ruins, unprotected from the storms of this life. When our hearts yearn for beauty, truth, and goodness, we are renewed inwardly by love.

25. Psalm 36:8–9.

Follow the signs pointing homeward along the paths of sacred reading. *Lectio divina,* also known as sacred reading, is an ancient practice of reflection upon Scripture, a practice found in chapter forty-eight of *The Rule of Saint Benedict.* Benedict calls his monks to meditate daily (Latin: *meditatio*) by slowly reading and reciting the words of Scripture. Benedictine scholar Terrance Kardong, OSB writes of this ancient way of meditation: "For the monks of this period, *meditatio* was not the silent intellectual exercise it is for us, but rather the verbal repetition of a memorized text."[26] As Paul encouraged Timothy, "Until I arrive, give attention to the public reading of scripture, to exhorting, to teaching."[27] A thousand years earlier, the psalmist declared the same wisdom: "Oh, how I love your law! It is my meditation all day long."[28]

We are wise not to neglect sacred reading, but diligently apply our minds and hearts to deepen our lives by drinking deeply from mountain streams of wisdom. When asked about a matter of the heart, we will be better equipped when we've already studied the question. Through daily sacred reading, we will be prepared to guide others without delay. As St. Peter encourages us, "Always be ready to make your defense to anyone who demands from you an accounting for the hope that is in you."[29]

The discipline of sacred reading calls us to arise from our daily duties, withdraw to "mountain streams," sit down for a time, and learn to fill our "water bottles" with eternal water. The labor of sacred reading is not pleasant at first, and many seek to avoid it, hoping a water faucet will show up along the way. Yet, through this ancient practice, we find our lives renewed, like quenching our thirst from a mountain stream.

The daily gift of sacred reading may be learned through four movements of our heart. First, we slowly read (*lectio*) a short passage of Scripture or other selection of wise writing. Second, we reflect (*meditatio*) upon those words by slowly rereading the passage, listening with the heart to the wisdom and truth found there. Third, we respond (*oratio*) by rereading the passage a third time, engaging our life personally through journaling or prayer or making action plans drawn from the passage. Finally, we rest (*contemplatio*) our mind and heart in the passage, allowing our life to sit

26. Kardong, *Benedict's Rule*, 170.

27. 1 Timothy 4:13.

28. Psalm 119:97.

29. 1 Peter 3:15.

quietly, learning the delight of sacred reading, the quiet labor of filtering refreshing wisdom into our lives.

As mentors, we help mentees fill their water bottles, taking time to fill their lives with wisdom, truth, and love. The ancient discipline of sacred reading is something like drinking from mountain streams. When we've done the fifteen-minute labor of sacred reading earlier in the day, we draw upon those "water bottles" later in the day, taking long draughts or quick sips for soul refreshment. Sacred reading, like drinking from a mountain stream, begins in our head, but quickly moves downward into our inner life, bringing refreshment, rejuvenation, and new life to our whole being.

We are journeying home together. We keep moving forward, drawn by the longing for home, motivated by love. As St. Paul writes, "For the love of Christ urges us on . . ."[30] Step by step, we journey on together, through storms, among ruins of this life, aware of the many distractions and dangers that are all around us, yet pressing on in our journey, fixing our lives on the goal ahead. We are refreshed and renewed daily in our journey of faith through the ancient practice of *lectio divina*. It readies us to offer guidance to other fellow travelers, to give answers from the hope that is in us. Like trail guides, we choose to walk alongside others in their journey, always pointing the way towards the high places of love where mountain streams flow.

Key to Mentoring

Like filling water bottles from mountain streams, we are wise to carry refreshment with us and help others quench their inner thirst through the daily practice of sacred reading.

Mentoring Inventory: Part Two

As we come to the end of Part Two of *Soul Mentoring*, I once again invite you to take a few moments to review Gregory's mentoring guidebook, considering ways you may deepen your life and develop as a soul mentor. Below you'll find a checklist, a mentoring inventory drawn from Part Two of Gregory's *Pastoral Care*. In each statement below, assess your experience

---

30. 2 Corinthians 5:14.

of soul care, either as a giver or receiver, and write in the left margin next to each statement the number that most describes where you are at this time:

3 – strongly agree & mostly true of me;

2 – somewhat agree & partially true of me;

1 – somewhat disagree & mostly not true of me.

- I strive to live with integrity, opening my life to be cleansed, centered, opened, shaped, filled, and used to help others live with integrity.

- I am learning to walk the talk, seeking daily to live according to the principles and ideals I profess with my lips, pressing on to live with integrity in all areas of my life.

- I am learning to live with wisdom in both silence and speech, keeping guard over my lips, listening more often, and speaking less often, knowing that words can easily be overlooked or lost when spoken in haste or without care.

- I desire to live a well-balanced life of contemplation and compassion, ascending into the heights of contemplation in order to descend into the valley to serve others with compassion.

- I am beginning to learn to balance kindness and strictness, grace and law, mercy and judgment, holding them together in the fire of the soul and forging them into mentoring tools to bring about healing and spiritual growth.

- I tend to see people from both the inside out and the outside in, and I am growing in my awareness of the inner and outer forces which promote or hinder growth in my life as well as in the lives of others.

- In all I do, I am motivated by love; I seek to mentor others in a life of love, helping them to discover deeper affection, truth, and love.

- With discernment and mutual respect, I am learning to gently remove my own masks as well as the masks of others, and I am allowing my life to be dressed with simplicity, generosity, compassion, responsibility, and wisdom.

- I know what a gift it is to receive mercy instead of judgment, acceptance instead of rejection, and grace instead of condemnation, in my own soul as well as in the lives of those I mentor.

- Like drinking from a mountain stream, I am learning the ancient practice of *lectio divina*, refreshing my life and the lives of others through daily sacred reading, reflection, personal response, and rest.

Count up your points. If you scored 21–30, you will serve well as a soul mentor for others. If you scored 11–20, you are developing many excellent traits for mentoring and have room for growth. If you scored 10 points or less, you are just beginning your journey into soul care and would benefit from having a mentor to help you in this journey.

Part Three

The Practice of Mentoring—Becoming a Skillful Musician[1]

I began playing the piano as a child. My parents took me to weekly piano lessons, bought me piano instruction books, and had me practice at home on our upright piano. During my early teen years, my dad taught me basics of jazz piano and I further developed my love of playing. I began exploring ways to express on the piano the music I heard playing in my soul. But it wasn't until I entered high school that I developed wings and began to learn to fly as a musician. I took weekly lessons with a good jazz pianist, learned the basics of jazz improvisation, and practiced daily with my high school jazz band. After years of musical training and experience, I've developed the ability to sit at a piano with no written music and paint the melody, harmony, and rhythm of the musical landscapes and moods of my soul.

Gregory opens Part Three of *Pastoral Care* by comparing a mentor to a skilled musician.

> If I may say so, what are the minds of an attentive audience if not the taut strings of a harp, which a skillful musician plays with multiple techniques so as to produce a melody, because even though

1. Each chapter in this section is based upon a chapter of *Pastoral Rule,* Part Three. My numbering of chapters does not directly correspond with Gregory's numbering. I've provided notations for readers to better connect quotations from *Pastoral Rule.*

they are played with one pick, they are not played with one type of stroke.[2]

As anyone who has played a musical instrument knows from experience, musical skill develops over time, over months and years. No one becomes a master musician the first day they pick up an instrument. Only by training, lessons, lots of practice, many mistakes, and many more hours of experience with an instrument does the beauty of the music develop. The same holds true for soul mentoring.

In Gregory's metaphor, the strings we play are the minds and hearts of people. We enter mentoring as beginners, like a person sitting down at a piano for the first time. Only over time, with training, being mentored ourselves, and hours of experience in mentoring can we expect to help another person play the beautiful melodies they are meant to play. To produce a beautiful sound, we learn "multiple techniques," treating every person as unique, as we skillfully learn to "produce a melody" from various types of people. As Gregory writes, "the discourse of the [mentor] should be adapted to the character of his audience so that it can address the specific needs of each individual and yet never shrink from the art of communal edification."[3] The goal is building up people—both individuals and communities of people—through mentoring.

In Part Three, Gregory lists forty pairs of opposites, unveiling an ancient catalogue of human personality types. He writes, "the same exhortation is not suited for everyone because not everyone shares the same quality of character."[4] If you are familiar with the Myers-Briggs Type Indicator, also known as the MBTI, you'll know this personality inventory consists of four pairs of opposites, resulting in sixteen personality types. I've tested as an ENFP, with preferences towards extraversion, intuition, feeling, and perceiving. Just as "the Myers-Briggs Type Indicator instrument can be a tool for personal growth, achieving balance, understanding self, and creating possibilities,"[5] so Gregory's forty pairs of opposites

2. Gregory, *Pastoral Rule*, 87–88.

3. Ibid., 87.

4. Ibid.

5. Quoted from the Myers & Briggs Foundation website at http://www.myersbriggs.org/type-use-for-everyday-life/type-in-personal-growth/ (accessed on July 15, 2014).

provide an excellent instrument for mentors and mentees to better understand the growth of the soul and find better balance in daily life.

Like the opening pages of a beginning piano instruction book, Part Three may seem irrelevant at first. Why not just skip the boring work of learning scales and jump right to the concert hall? Gregory unveils the ancient art of soul mentoring in this section by helping his readers better understanding the many strings that make up the grand instrument of humanity. His musical instrument of choice, the harp, like the piano, consists of many strings. Becoming a skillful musician, like becoming a skillful mentor, requires hours of study, developing a greater and greater ability to bring out the beautiful melodies of those we mentor by better understanding each mentee's unique "quality of character." Gregory encourages mentors to build others up in love, touching the hearts of mentees with the same basic understanding of human nature, yet approaching each person as a unique soul requiring a unique approach to mentoring.

Gregory concludes Part Three by returning to his first picture of mentoring as a path along which we walk together, mentor and mentee, like two friends walking together along the beach at sunset.

> The footprint of . . . good living should be that path that others follow rather than the sound of his voice showing them where to go. . . . Before they offer any words of exhortation, they should proclaim by their actions everything that they wish to say.[6]

Faithful mentors walk their talk, putting into action the very wisdom of life and love they seek to build into the lives of those they are mentoring. In the following pages, we will follow Gregory's model of mentoring by reviewing his forty pairs of opposites, considering the unique ways of building others up in love as a "skillful musician," employing "multiple techniques" for each unique person. We are more remembered for how we live than by what we say. As we consider the best approach to mentoring, Gregory reminds us that in soul mentoring we must be like skillful musicians making beautiful music together with others.

6. Gregory, *Pastoral Rule*, 207.

CHAPTER 21

Men and Women[7]

Gregory opens Part Three with gender differences, calling us to be attentive to the unique traits of men and women. While there is always a risk of stereotyping gender differences, we are wise to think about qualities of being male or female when we are seeking a mentor or caring for a mentee. In my experience, men are best mentored by men, and women by women. In general, men understand each other, and women understand women in ways men cannot. Each gender wrestles with burdens in their own unique way.

Men often shoulder heavy loads without seeking anyone to help carry their burden. Mentoring is one way to relieve the heavy load upon a man. Yet mentors should not avoid calling a man to carry the burden of responsibility for his own choices and intentions, or to step up to the heavier burden of learning to care for others.

While women usually carry lighter physical loads than men, women often balance more demands and challenges than men. Often in society today, mothers carry the dual load of full-time work outside the home and providing for full-time care of children. Recently I heard a report about maternity and paternity benefits in Sweden. While Swedish mothers are using 75 percent of their maternity leave, only 30 percent of paternity leave is being used by fathers. In one of the most progressive countries in the world, men still leave most of the full-time care of children to women, preferring to go back to work outside the home even when being paid by their government to stay at home as full-time fathers.[8] Writing in a time when women were often overlooked and devalued by society, we can appreciate Gregory's sensitivity toward gender, calling men to carry their load while encouraging mentors to care for women "with gentleness."[9]

---

7. This chapter comes from Gregory's *Pastoral Rule*, III.2.

8. See http://www.npr.org/blogs/babyproject/2011/08/09/139121410/parental-leave -the-swedes-are-the-most-generous, (accessed on July 1, 2014).

9. Gregory, *Pastoral Rule*, 90.

CHAPTER 22

Young and Old[10]

Gregory seeks the best way to encourage progress in life for each individual person according to their unique place in life, including age. Adults often feel uncomfortable around youth and prefer to let electronic diversions or varieties of electronic entertainment substitute for person-to-person mentoring. Gregory knows better: he calls adult mentors to lead youth to life improvements through "strict admonition." Kids need challenges. We need not be afraid of offering them the gift of loving discipline, measurable targets for growth, and accountability when they miss the mark. At the other end of life, the elderly are best mentored by "gentle reminders." Ask questions about their history, and give them the gift of your ears and heart, listening with them for the wisdom of decades, as they tell you their life story, as a wise grandmother shares her heart with her granddaughter. As written long ago, "Do not speak harshly to an older man, but speak to him as to a father, to younger men as brothers, to older women as mothers, to younger women as sisters–with absolute purity."[11]

CHAPTER 23

Poor and Rich[12]

The gap between the poor and the rich continues to widen. According to a feature story on National Public Radio on July 10, 2011, "The income gap in the United States has ballooned: It's wider than any time since 1928, in the days before the stock market crash triggered the Great Depression." At the time of that story, the Federal Reserve Governor, Sarah Bloom

10. This chapter also comes from *Pastoral Rule*, III.2.

11. 1 Timothy 5:1–2.

12. This chapter also comes from *Pastoral Rule*, III.2.

Raskin stated, "This inequality is destabilizing and undermines the ability of the economy to grow sustainably and efficiently. Income inequality is anathema to the social progress that is part and parcel of such growth."[13] As a middle class American, I've always been humbled when I've traveled among the poor, either in United States or in other countries. I've been warmly welcomed into homes with dirt floors, and discovered hearts of gratitude, joy, and generosity among the poor. When I return home and hold up the mirror to my own soul, I ask where I am finding my highest treasure: in material possessions, or in the richness of faith, hope, and love.

Gregory wisely paints with broad brushstrokes the differences between the poor and the rich. The poor often possess unseen wealth of humility and depth of character, while the rich often trust in "the uncertainty of riches," like grasping handfuls of sand at the beach. According to the New Testament, it is not money that gets us into trouble, but our attitude towards wealth. "For the love of money is a root of all kinds of evil, and in their eagerness to be rich some have wandered away from the faith and pierced themselves with many pains."[14] The more we seek to possess visible wealth, the more such fleeting forms of wealth possess us. Though some, like Francis of Assisi, voluntarily enter a life of poverty, most people do not chose a life of poverty, but would prefer a life of financial independence. Yet the greater our need for life's essentials, the more we look up for help and the more we grow in gratitude for the priceless gifts money cannot buy, such as laughter, music, sunshine, love, and good friends.

Gregory also offers qualifiers: some poor people struggle with selfishness, while some rich people live in true humility. A wise mentor looks behind the curtain of financial wealth to seek the true wealth of a person's character. The heart of mentoring has little to do with bank accounts or income, and everything to do with heart accounts of expanding a person's capacity for love of God and goodwill towards others.

Thus, when mentoring the poor, offer comfort in the face of hardships. When mentoring the rich, warn people against putting their trust in what is unstable. As the Good Book instructs, "As for those who in the present age are rich, command them not to be haughty, or to set their hopes

13. See http://www.npr.org/2011/07/10/137744694/as-income-gap-balloons-is-it-holding-back-growth, (accessed on July 1, 2014).

14. 1 Timothy 6:10.

on the uncertainty of riches, but rather on God who richly provides us with everything for our enjoyment."[15]

The poor often possess unseen wealth, such as character of the heart, while the rich sometimes vainly grasp at visible wealth like someone trying to catch the wind in their hands. Of course, there are arrogant people among the poor, and humble people among the rich. In such cases, a mentor is wise to adapt words that best fit the inner character of the mentee, gently encouraging those who are humble, and firmly challenging those who are arrogant. Some wounds can only be healed with gentle care, while other diseases must be cut out with the skill and confidence of a wise surgeon.

CHAPTER 24

Joyful and Sad [16]

I love the saying by British explorer Sir Ranulph Fiennes, "There is no such thing as bad weather, only inappropriate clothing."[17] People generally love talking about the weather. Rain or shine, chilly or warm, the weather is one of the most reliable subjects for discussion among strangers. We are all surrounded by the forces of nature, and each person responds in their own way to the weather.

Gregory believed in appropriate mentoring no matter the weather of the soul. Wise mentors care for happy souls differently than sad souls. Soul weather can be an outer expression of an inward temperament, or an internal response to external circumstances. When external circumstances are "sunny," we tend to feel better about ourselves and others. But when outside forces turn dark and stormy, we easily get down and can cast dark shadows on those around us. Regarding the more permanent nature of a human soul, some people seem to have a perpetually sunny disposition, a warm-weather temperament. Others tend towards a cloudy temperament, with an

15. 1 Timothy 6:17.

16. This chapter is based upon *Pastoral Rule,* III.3. All subsequent chapters in this section are based upon the next sequential chapter in *Pastoral Rule,* until we reach chapter 37–38, which I've combined.

17. Brandreth, *Oxford Dictionary of Humorous Quotations,* 319.

overcast soul often troubled by dark thoughts or depression. The Hundred Acre Wood has plenty of room for both Tigger and Eeyore. To those like Tigger, who always have a bounce in their step and sunshine in their soul, Gregory encourages mentors to set before their eyes the needs of others, that they may grow in compassion for them. Help the happy to learn to mourn, for the voice of truth spoke from ancient times, "Blessed are those who mourn for they will be comforted."[18] But with those who inwardly suffer under cloudy skies, Gregory writes: "Before the sad the joyous promises of the kingdom should be set."[19] People who are by nature melancholic need constant reminders of the dawning light which comes to those living in the land of shadows. As Luke writes,

> By the tender mercy of our God,
>
> the dawn from on high will break upon us,
>
> to give light to those who sit in darkness and in the shadow of death,
>
> to guide our feet into the way of peace.[20]

CHAPTER 25

Leaders and Followers

As a child, I loved playing the game follow-the-leader with my brothers. I loved being a follower, with my oldest brother in the lead. Wherever he climbed we would climb. When he jumped, we too would jump. When he acted like a baboon, we too acted like baboons. Often this game would take us into places I otherwise would have never attempted to go to. Mentoring takes us where we might otherwise not choose to go.

As a wise mentor, Gregory speaks to followers differently than to leaders. With followers, we hear a gentle voice lifting up those who are crushed under the demands of harsh leaders. Gregory calls followers to offer their lives in humility, submitting to the leaders over them, and stepping up to complete the tasks asked of them by those in charge. Followers are advised

---

18. Matthew 5:3.

19. Gregory, *Pastoral Rule*, 93.

20. Luke 1:78.

"not to judge the lives of their leaders too quickly, even when they witness reprehensible actions."[21] How easy to jump to judgment when we do not have the heavy burden of leadership upon our shoulders. So Gregory asks followers keep watch over their attitudes and inner thoughts, and to make adjustments in the ways we consider those in positions of power. He calls followers to be constrained and moderate in criticism of leaders, asking followers to take responsibility for their lives and avoid laziness. He quotes an ancient proverb: "Go to the ant, you lazybones; consider its ways and be wise."[22] Followers are wise to regularly inspect their heart motives, asking themselves, "Are there ways in my life that I fail to accept authority?" The relationship between a leader and a group of followers rests upon mutual respect and trust. So followers are encouraged to support their leaders and not be too quick to judge the lives of those in power.

On the other hand, Gregory has more to say to those in leadership than to those who follow. He calls leaders to "preside with moderation," warning them against becoming filled with pride or provoking those they lead with anger. Rather, leaders are to live "in such a way as to provide a good example."[23] This again illustrates two basic principles of Gregory's way: leading by example and walking the talk. As Gregory writes, a leader is "compelled to satisfy in deed what he instructs others to do with his voice"[24]—in other words, live with integrity. Gregory calls leaders to live vigilantly, keeping alert to the needs and troubles of those under their care. He quotes from an ancient proverb, "Do not give rest to your eyes, nor let your eyelids slumber," commenting on this bit of wisdom, "To give rest to the eyes is to cease attentiveness, so as to neglect altogether the care of subordinates."[25] Wise leaders, like excellent teachers, have "eyes all around," looking both within themselves and into the lives of those they lead, so "they can detect what should be corrected in others."[26]

21. Gregory, *Pastoral Rule*, 95.
22. Proverbs 6:6.
23. Gregory, *Pastoral Rule*, 93–94.
24. Ibid., 95.
25. Ibid., quoting Proverbs 6:3–4.
26. Ibid.

CHAPTER 26

Employees and Employers

Watching our kids play video games during their childhood, I wondered how they would relate to the adult working world. One of the most common terms for the big, bad enemy in video gaming lingo is "boss." When the boss is always bad, and the hero is the little guy who conquers all the bosses, there may be some negative connotations later in life when confronted with a real-life boss in a real-life job. I've enjoyed observing the healthy relationships our grown sons have with their real-life bosses at their places of employment.

Gregory writes of mentoring among employers and employees. In doing so, he is about 1,400 years ahead of his time with his best-selling book in Europe on leadership and organizational mentoring. Many of the latest best-selling mentoring books are aimed at business leaders relating better with their employees and customers. Gregory uses the sixth-century language of master and servant, but the meaning is similar to what we think of today as employer and employee.

In the ancient world, as today, there were those in charge and those "under the yoke."[27] Gregory tells employees to "consider the humility of their position," while telling employers they "should not forget that they share the same condition" as those under their charge. Unlike many people in power today, Gregory highly valued the virtue of humility, one of the leading virtues of Benedictine spirituality. The longest chapter in *The Rule of Benedict*, chapter seven, is on humility, offering a twelve-step approach to entering into this upside-down way of life, a way of life very familiar to Gregory. Of all the possible titles Gregory could have chosen when elected to the high office of bishop of Rome, he chose "servant of the servants of God." In essence, Gregory understood leadership to be an act of service, and leaders as those tasked with lifting up and caring for those under their charge.

27. Ibid., 97.

Applying this point of view to leaders, Gregory advises "that they know that they are the fellow servants of their servants."[28] Yet, Gregory also warns those without power to respect the boss, quoting St. Paul in his letter to a young mentee, Timothy: "Let as many servants as are under the yoke consider their masters to be worthy of all honor." Put into today's language, "All you employees, consider your boss as worthy of honor." To employers, corporate bosses, company leaders, and managers, Gregory asks you to do the same, to consider your workers "to be worthy of honor," and to treat all people with dignity and respect, knowing the one true Boss is looking down upon earthly employers and employees from heaven, empowering both to live to their fullest potential.

CHAPTER 27

The Educated and the Uneducated

While the United States celebrates literacy rates of 99 percent, illiteracy continues to trouble millions of people around the world. In parts of Africa, such as in Burkina Faso, only one in four people can read. So when I look back on my formal education spanning twenty-four years of my life, I'm amazed at the gift of classroom learning I've been given. I love to read, study, and learn. When Gregory writes about mentoring the educated and uneducated, he gets my attention. Those of us who have devoted much of our lives to education, including the pursuit of degrees, may find it strange to read that we should "ignore what [we] know," and also that we should "eradicate the notion that [we] are intelligent."[29] Is Gregory down on intelligence and knowledge? No, but he is aware of inherent troubles among the well-educated.

From Gregory's perspective, the educated are vulnerable to arrogance, thinking they are better than the uneducated. As declared long ago, "Knowledge puffs up, but love builds up."[30] So Gregory encourages mentors

28. Ibid.
29. Ibid.
30. 1 Corinthians 8:1.

to help the educated "become more wisely foolish and to learn the wise foolishness of God."[31] This advice is something like telling a person with a PhD to go back to high school as a sophomore, as a wise fool, admitting they do not know very much, still need to learn, and be taught like all the rest of us. Gregory tells the educated to "advance in what the world considers foolishness, for this is true wisdom."[32]

Though Gregory does not give examples of how to live out such advice, we can pencil in a few possibilities in the margin. First, spend more time with children. Learn from a child how to play. Get on the floor with a child and watch them, listen to them, and let them guide you back into the wisdom of childhood.

Second, learn a new language. Ask a native speaker of some language other than English to be your language tutor and meet weekly to learn that language. Or sign up for a community college class in that language, and go back to school to learn.

Third, travel to another country, and ask a local to tell you about their way of life. Eat their food. Listen to their indigenous music. Become a learner in a foreign culture.

Finally, spend time in a place very different that where you normally live. If you are a "country mouse," go to the big city. If you are a "city mouse," spend time in a rural place. Paul invites us to advance in "foolishness" when he writes, "If you think that you are wise in this age, you should become fools so that you may become wise."[33]

As for the uneducated, mentors should encourage them "to learn what they do not know" and encourage them in "whatever is known of heavenly wisdom."[34] There is a form of literacy that cannot be learned in public schools, or even schools like Stanford. Transport a magna cum laude graduate of Harvard into a jungle in Papau New Guinea, and watch the uneducated and illiterate locals outsmart Mr. Ivy League all day long with their survival skills. "God chose what is foolish in the world to shame the wise; God chose what is weak in the world to shame the strong . . ."[35] While the educated are most influenced by knowledge and reason, the uneducated

31. Gregory, *Pastoral Rule*, 98.
32. Ibid.
33. 1 Corinthians 3:18.
34. Gregory, *Pastoral Rule*, 98.
35. 1 Corinthians 1:27.

are best mentored by "the gentle force of example."[36] Gregory encourages mentors to share with those who have little or no formal education "the praiseworthy acts of others," so that they may learn by example and "arise to higher things" by the way of wisdom.[37]

CHAPTER 28

The Bold and the Shy

For the past three decades I've acted in more than a dozen plays and musicals at our local community theater, including *My Fair Lady, Hello Dolly, The Foreigner, The Christmas Carol,* and *You Can't Take It With You.* I've played supporting roles and leading roles. No matter the role, getting in front of a live audience requires a measure of boldness and self-confidence. Oddly, I am not naturally a bold person. Many of the other actors I've worked with on the stage are also reserved, introverted people. For some reason, many naturally shy or modest people love to dress up, memorize scripts, and step onstage before a live audience to invite others into the magic of theater.

Gregory realized there are many types of actors on the stage of life. Some leading actors love the spotlight and step confidently into center stage. Others prefer playing supporting roles, willing to say less and be less noticed. With the leads, a mentor needs to lead: be bold with the bold. The best directors I've worked under while playing a lead role were very direct, calling out stage directions, stopping bad acting by telling the actor face-to-face that their acting needs improvement, and offering few (if any) words of encouragement. Those in lead positions with boldness of character need clear, direct correction from a mentor and will have greater respect for a director of the soul who tells them honestly what needs to be changed. As Gregory writes, the bold are "better corrected with direct accusations."[38]

---

36. Gregory, *Pastoral Rule,* 99.
37. Ibid., 98.
38. Ibid., 99.

On the contrary, those who are in supporting roles are "more easily corrected by a modest exhortation . . . as if a gentle pat."[39] Most people respond well to gentle reminders and encouragement. "Support" people, who tend towards shyness, are accustomed to receiving guidance from those in charge, and normally do not require any strictness in guidance. Mentors who use kindness and compassion with shy people practice the ancient wisdom of Gregory, who writes, "gentle speech covers the mistakes of the modest."[40]

CHAPTER 29

The Assertive and the Timid

After three decades of leading small groups, including leadership teams, prayer groups, and home study groups, I've come to accept that some will hide in the corner, saying nothing, while others step boldly into the middle to dominate the conversation. One home group I led years ago disbanded after half a dozen painful meetings where one person insisted on talking most of the time. Several in the group, myself included, tried to work with this person to help them learn to let others to participate, but to no avail. When attempting to nurture healthy communities among small groups, one of the biggest challenges is learning to tactfully settle the assertive while gently drawing out the timid.

How do you mentor assertive people, those who "govern themselves" and "presume that everything they do is of singular importance"?[41] How do you correct those who "despise being corrected by others"?[42] How do you help those who seek only to please themselves? How does a mentor best help others out of a life of vice into a life of virtue?

These are the types of questions Gregory brings up in his *Pastoral Care*, Part Three. "Sometimes . . . they are least aware that they are guilty of

39. Ibid.
40. Ibid.
41. Ibid., 100.
42. Ibid.

the vice of forwardness."[43] Wise mentors hold up a mirror of truth to help mentees see themselves more clearly. We do this by asking good questions that help a mentee search his or her heart motives. We also do this by taking an active interest in a mentee's life. The more we live in the light of love, the more that light will reflect upon the mentees who are caught up in the shadows of self-centeredness.

There are others who are timid in their approach to life, unsure of themselves, "too conscious of their weaknesses," and are prone to "fall into despair" or "break down from despondency."[44] For the timid, mentors are wise to point out to them the good character already present in their lives. As Gregory writes, "the hearing of praise may nourish their tenderness."[45] Any exhortation of the timid is best offered gently, with plenty of praise, words of praise that may "settle their minds so that they would not be shaken by admonition."[46] Dorothy Law Nolte wrote this wisdom into a beautiful poem titled "Children Learn What They Live":.

> If a child lives with encouragement, he learns to be confident . . .
> If a child lives with praise, he learns to be appreciative.
> If a child lives with acceptance, he learns to love . . .
> With what is your child living?[47]

CHAPTER 30

The Impatient and the Patient

We live in a fast-paced world. During the past few decades, the digital revolution has pushed the Western world faster and faster, deflating the value society places upon the classic virtue of patience. How do you respond when you have to wait a few extra seconds for something to load on your

43. Ibid.
44. Ibid.
45. Ibid., 101.
46. Ibid.
47. Nolte, *Children Learn What They Live*, 107.

computer? Or what is your immediate response as you are making a phone call when a computer voice tells you to hold for the next available agent? Soul mentors learn to care for both impatient and patient people.

Gregory commends patient people, describing them as tranquil and innocent in their hearts. From Gregory's experience, patient people learn more easily, love more freely, and serve others more selflessly, even when it hurts to do so. One of the Greek words for patience, *hupomeno*, literally translated means "to remain under," or to hang in there; as though someone tried to knock you off the tightrope, and you still hang on upside down. The patient way of life is something of an upside-down way of living in the midst of fast-food restaurants, high-speed computers, flash trading on the stock market, fast lanes on freeways, smart phones, instant messaging, and other impatient expressions of our hurry-up world. But patient people are also vulnerable to self-pity, allowing themselves to be crushed under the demands and weights of people in a hurry. "Therefore, the patient should be told to study how to tolerate those whom it is necessary for them to love," writes Gregory.[48] Mentoring is slow, thoughtful work that asks both mentors and mentees to exercise the virtue of patience.

On the contrary, Gregory offers many warnings against the curse of impatience. "The impatient . . . are carried into many types of iniquity that they do not desire, because clearly impetuousness drives the mind where it does not want to go."[49] Through impatience, people "act hastily as a result of their emotions," becoming confused, full of regret, and angry. Ultimately, impatient people give up on love. "Love is patient; love is kind," declares St. Paul in his famous love chapter.[50] According to Gregory, the impatient lose possession of their souls by letting go of love. "When patience is minimal, charity does not exist."[51] Better to suffer a little sacrifice with love than race down the fast lane full of frustration and impatience.

Over the past few decades, a global "Slow Movement" has emerged, beginning with the slow food movement in the late eighties, and subsequently growing to incorporate more and more aspects of our fast-paced world. The Slow Movement encourages people to seek a slower pace of life with more connection and intention, through such diverse arenas as slow gardening, slow travel, slow education, slow parenting, slow technology,

48. Gregory, *Pastoral Rule*, 104.
49. Ibid., 102.
50. 1 Corinthians 13:4.
51. Gregory, *Pastoral Rule*, 102.

and even slow church.[52] Love keeps inviting us to slow down, to learn to live more in the present than the past or future, and to slowly grow the fruit of patience. As Richard Carlson and Joseph Bailey affirm, "Discover for yourself that life can be enjoyable, that it can be easier than you imagined, and that you can actually slow down to a very sane pace . . . to slow down to the pace of life. If you can, the quality of your life will be greatly enhanced."[53]

CHAPTER 31

The Generous and the Envious

In his classic book *Mere Christianity*, C. S. Lewis invites us to consider the nature of a truly humble person:

> Do not imagine that if you meet a really humble man he will be what most people call 'humble' nowadays: he will not be a sort of greasy, smarmy person, who is always telling you that, of course, he is a nobody. Probably all you will think about him is that he seemed a cheerful, intelligent chap who took a real interest in what *you* said to *him*. If you do dislike him it will be because you feel a little envious of anyone who seems to enjoy life so easily.[54]

How do you feel when you meet someone who takes a real interest in your life? How envious are you around others who enjoy life easily? When you see others succeed, how easy or difficult is it for you to celebrate their success? When you've worked together with others on a project and someone else in the group gets most of the credit, how do you respond? When people you distrust or dislike perform acts of kindness, how hard is it to offer your praise for their deeds? Where would you put yourself along the line between generosity and envy?

Gregory calls soul mentors to shine the light of love into the hearts of mentees, to discern those who are generous and those who are envious. Generous people "co-celebrate the good in others as much as they wish to

52. See Smith and Pattison, *Slow Church*.
53 Carlson and Bailey, *Slowing Down to the Speed of Life*, 10.
54. Lewis, *Mere Christianity*, 101.

have the same good for themselves."[55] When people have a kindly nature, they tend to think well of others, and "lovingly praise the deeds of their neighbors in the hope that they multiply them by imitation."[56] With such people, encourage the art of imitation, that the good in others will be multiplied in the life of the mentee. Celebrate with those who celebrate. Rejoice with those who rejoice. Offer praise with those who are being praised.

As we shine the light of love into human hearts, we will meet envious hearts who do not rejoice in the good found in others, but become troubled when they see others prosper. Envy blinds the soul, consumes us with an inner burning of what we do not have, and leaves us in a state of decay. As the ancient proverb asserts, "A heart at peace gives life to the body, but envy rots the bones."[57] With the envious, point out the excellent character of charity found among the generous, "which makes the labor of others our own without any work on our part."[58] As Lewis writes, encourage the envious to learn to step outside themselves by taking a real interest in what others say.

Gregory presents an ancient view of the human community as a "single body," a picture which may help mentors and mentees learn to become more generous of heart. Like the human body, we are interlinked, diverse yet one. We belong together. "The foot sees by the eyes, and through the foot, the eyes move . . . the stomach supports the hands, and the hands work for the stomach."[59] Gregory draws upon a metaphor from Paul's First Letter to the Corinthians, where Paul compares the faith community to a human body. "God arranged the members in the body, each one of them, as he chose. If all were a single member, where would the body be? As it is, there are many members, yet one body."[60] Just as various parts of our physical bodies rely upon other parts and benefit from their unique role, so we too may learn to rely upon other parts of the human community around us, benefiting from others' unique gifts and talents instead of envying what we do not have. Gregory reassures us when he writes, "Those good qualities that we love in others, which we do not seem to be able to imitate, are, in fact, ours also. And whatever is loved in us becomes the possession of those

55. Gregory, *Pastoral Rule*, 107.
56. Ibid.
57. Proverbs 14:30, quoted from the NIV.
58. Gregory, *Pastoral Rule*, 108.
59. Ibid.
60. Ibid. See 1 Corinthians 12:18–20.

who love them."[61] In this way, we learn to live our lives more generously, cheerfully, and easily.

CHAPTER 32

The Sincere and the Insincere

I live in a rainy climate with more grey days than blue skies. When the sun shines, we head outside to soak in the glory. Humans need light. Without sunlight we perish. In Greek, the word for sincerity combines the word for sunlight, *heli,* with the word "to judge," *krineas.*[62] To live with sincerity is to live in the light, allowing our lives to be evaluated by the light. There are people though who prefer to live in darkness, including the darkness of ignorance, unbelief, self-deception, and insincerity.

Gregory encourages soul mentors to guide mentees into the light, to help reveal the inner character of the mentee, so that those we seek to guide may see more clearly their true nature. He urges mentors to praise the sincere for their love of truth, their intent to speak the truth, and for "being careful not to say anything false."[63] But he also advises sincere people to remain silent at times, for "hearing the truth can be harmful," and to only offer the truth "when it is appropriate."[64] As Jesus taught, we are to be "wise as serpents and innocent as doves."[65] Gregory seeks to guard the innocence of the sincere, knowing attacks that can come from powerful, corrupt people. Those living in darkness often do not like the light of truth shining in their faces, even when it is the gentle light of dawn.

To the insincere, Gregory warns that "falsehood always harms the one who speaks it."[66] People often hide under multiple layers of falsehoods, afraid others may discover their duplicity. Mentors are wise to realize that

---

61. Ibid.
62. *Eilikrineas.*
63. Gregory, *Pastoral Rule,* 110.
64. Ibid.
65. Matthew 10:16.
66. Gregory, *Pastoral Rule,* 110.

some mentees will be drawn "into a defensive posture" when the mentor shines the light of truth upon their souls. Such a mentee may choose to hide "in the obscurity of self-defense."[67] Insincere people put up false defenses and become troubled by fearful suspicions, though they may not realize it. Gregory describes insincere people as "being led astray by the mists of falsehood."[68] I've heard of mountain climbers or backpackers on exposed ridges becoming lost in the wilderness simply because they headed off in the wrong direction, sometimes to their death, when they got confused in the fog, thinking they were heading back to camp. Living in the fog of insincerity takes a lot of energy. "How heavy the load of duplicity," and how easy to become "wearied from the endeavor," laments Gregory.[69]

Better to walk in the light, as Jesus encourages: "Walk while you have the light, so that the darkness may not overtake you. If you walk in the darkness, you do not know where you are going. While you have the light, believe in the light, so that you may become children of light."[70] Humans, like most living things, require light to live. Like heliotropic plants that naturally turn toward the sun, we too have an inner compass which turns our souls toward the light, especially when a mentor gently guides us with radiance and the illumination of love.

CHAPTER 33

The Healthy and the Sick

Almost half of all Americans make New Year's resolutions, and it comes as no surprise that physical health resolutions lead the way. Every year, our top New Year's resolutions involve either losing weight, staying fit, or giving up smoking.[71] Who would disagree with the resolve to live a healthier life?

67. Ibid., 112.

68. Ibid., 111.

69. Ibid., 110.

70. John 12:35–36.

71. See http://www.statisticbrain.com/new-years-resolution-statistics/ (accessed on July 1, 2014).

While our first associations for health and sickness are physical, health involves our whole being, including mind, body, and spirit. What does a healthy mind and healthy soul look like? What is mental health and how can we better care for those with mental illnesses? How can we increase our spiritual health or avoid spiritual ills? Mentors are wise to consider such questions alongside those they mentor.

Gregory encourages the healthy to "exercise the health of the body for the benefit of the health of the soul."[72] To stop smoking is a worthy resolution, but removing a bad habit is easier when replacing it with a good habit for the improvement of one's soul. For example, quit smoking in order to have more breath to offer words of encouragement to others this year. Words of praise require lung power. Every time an ex-smoker gets the yearning to light up, a mentor could have them write down words of encouragement to speak to a friend or family member. Another example may be to lose weight in order to gain gratitude by offering thanks to God more often this year. Gratitude and praise are healthy habits of the soul.

The ancient art of soul mentoring encourages others to establish healthy habits which will please God, benefit their souls, and build up the lives of others. Gregory warns, "If they are not willing to please God when they are able, they will not be able to please him when they want."[73] God gives us healthy bodies, minds, and spirits to help us live our lives more fully for the sake of others. "When health that has been granted for doing good works is despised, only after it has been lost will one recognize how generous it was."[74]

Though nobody likes to be sick, sickness can also greatly benefit our souls. While lying in bed sick, we have time to reflect upon our lives and examine our souls. Gregory encourages mentors to advise the sick "to consider how beneficial bodily affliction can be, because it both cleanses sins already committed and prevents others from being accomplished."[75] The potential healing power of illness is an overlooked force in our daily lives. We strive hard for physical wellness, often forgetting that illness can be a wise guide along the pathway towards wholeness.

In the English language, the words "wholeness" and "holiness" come from the same etymological root. The Latin root word for health, *salus*,

72. Gregory, *Pastoral Rule*, 113.
73. Ibid.
74. Ibid., 114.
75. Ibid., 117.

refers to health, salvation, safety, well-being, and deliverance. In the Greek language, the words for health and salvation also come from the same root.[76] Only recently have we separated physical health from spiritual health, over-emphasizing physical wellness while neglecting the health of our souls. The ancient art of soul mentoring is holistic, seeing both health and sickness as guides along the way to holiness and wholeness. At the core of the good news sent by God we discover Jesus, who was wounded to bring us healing, offering God's gift of holiness and wholeness, salvation and health to all who are willing to follow in his steps.[77]

CHAPTER 34

The Sensitive and the Hardened

Sweet the rain's new fall, sunlit from heaven,
Like the first dewfall, on the first grass,
Praise for the sweetness of the wet garden,
Sprung in completeness where his feet pass.[78]

I live on the Oregon coast in a temperate rain forest. The coastal village where I live averages seventy-six inches of rain annually, which is exactly my height— that's six feet, four inches of rain. Where we live, the ground beneath our feet is almost always wet and soft. The dominate color surrounding our home is green. Evergreen trees soar high overhead, and sword ferns, salal, salmon berries, mosses, and may lilies grow below, along with hundreds of other patterns of green. Soil seldom has the chance to dry out or become hard in our climate.

In Italy, where Gregory spent most of his life, there is no lack of sunshine. Farmers work hard in dry climates to prepare the soil for planting. Hard soil is plowed up. Rocky soil is cleared of stones. Seeds are planted and

76. The Greek nouns for savior, *soter*, and salvation, *soterias*, both come from the Greek root *sozo*, meaning "to save, to heal, to make well, to rescue, to deliver."

77. See Isaiah 53:5 and 1 Peter 2:21–24.

78. "Morning Has Broken" by Eleanor Farjeon, in *Hymns for the Living Church*, 553.

watered. The miracle of life springs forth, requiring even more work such as weeding, thinning, pruning, watering, fertilizing, and harvesting.

The human soul may be compared to a garden or a field, with various types of soils, including soft and hard. One of Jesus's best-loved stories features a farmer sowing seed in his field.[79] Some of the seed falls on hard soil that has been trampled by feet. Some of the seed falls on rocky soil. Some of the seed falls on soil where weeds and thorns are growing. Finally, some of the seed falls on good soil. The growth of fruit is only evident in the last type of soil. Likewise, for various reasons, much of the good seed sown in the human heart never bears fruit.

Gregory tells mentors to care for sensitive hearts differently than hardened hearts.[80] People with softened soil "live innocently," and are "growing in the grace of love by nurturing charity."[81] Sometimes though, sensitive people may find their hearts motivated by fear rather than love. "There is no fear in love, but perfect love casts out fear; for fear has to do with punishment, and whoever fears has not reached perfection in love."[82] Wise mentors who discover a spirit of fear among those of sensitive heart will encourage them to live in love, allowing the love of God to fall upon them like the rain.

There are also those who live with "greater insensitivity," "who have become so hardened . . . that they cannot be corrected . . ."[83] Gregory laments the state of such a human heart, asserting, "sometimes those who remain unmoved by harsh punishments can be amended with sweet admonitions."[84] Through gentle encouragement and love, a well-trusted mentor may be able to soften even the hardest heart with the quiet rain of grace.

> Tis the gift to be loving, tis the best gift of all,
> Like a quiet rain it blesses where it falls,
> And with it we will truly believe,
> Tis better to give than it is to receive.[85]

79. See Mark 4:1–20.

80. Gregory, *Pastoral Rule*, 118 (3.13).

81. Ibid., 118.

82. 1 John 4:18.

83. Gregory, *Pastoral Rule*, 118.

84. Ibid., 121.

85. See http://en.wikipedia.org/wiki/Simple_Gifts (accessed July 7, 2014).

CHAPTER 35

The Silent and the Talkers

We live in a word-weary world. Daily our ears are inundated with words from electronic tablets, computers, cell phones, televisions, books, magazines, loudspeakers, and people. Except while we sleep, we rarely escape this outpouring of words. There are those rare people who speak very little. Silent people, like cloistered nuns, are for the most part overlooked. Occasionally they gain respect in a wordy world, though they're viewed as oddities. But the silent ones also have their troubles.

Gregory warns silent people against bridling the tongue unnecessarily, and hiding their vices behind their silence. Better to bring out into the open those hidden troubles, lest they "develop a greater pain because they do not speak about what they endure."[86] When we share our troubles with another person, "the pain that burns internally is released, the wound is opened for healing."[87] As the psalmist writes,

> While I kept silence, my body wasted away
> through my groaning all day long.
> For day and night your hand was heavy upon me;
> my strength was dried up as by the heat of summer.[88]

Not all silence is golden. Some forms of silence can be harmful to our health, eating us from within. "By the medicine of the voice, both parties can receive healing."[89] The one who caused the trouble may be kept from harming others; and the one who was hurt "is relieved by releasing his wound."[90]

Medicine is not the only helpful metaphor Gregory employs in describing how we should our words. He also speaks of the human soul as a walled city and as a water reservoir. Just as a walled city is guarded by the

---

86. Gregory, *Pastoral Rule*, 122.
87. Ibid.
88. Psalm 32:3–4.
89. Gregory, *Pastoral Rule*, 122.
90. Ibid.

thickness and height of its walls, so our lives may be guarded by "a wall of silence." Just as ancient walled cities kept watchmen by the gates, so we are wise to keep watch over our mouths, and carefully learn "when speech should open the mouth with discretion and when silence should keep it closed."[91] Gregory offers up an ancient prayer from the book of Psalms: "Set a guard over my mouth, O Lord; keep watch over the door of my lips."[92]

The human soul may also be viewed as a water reservoir. "When it is enclosed, it rises to higher levels because it seeks again the height from which it first descended." Thus, keeping silent allows us to ponder what is higher, renewing our lives with living water from God. When we speak, we open the gates of the reservoir, dispersing our inner waters. When our words are being put to good use to irrigate the lives of others, we should let them flow freely. But Gregory warns those who speak too frequently, comparing them to someone who opens the gates of a water reservoir without thinking of the consequences, thus making them slaves to "excessive speaking."[93] "They slip into excessive wordiness," and "the meaningless words that are wasted are like many streams that flow from themselves."[94] James encourages us to "be quick to listen, slow to speak, slow to anger."[95] Our words have the power to heal or destroy, to help or harm, to bring renewal or weariness. As a person who uses many words each week in my work as a pastor, I need the gift of silence to restore my soul and balance my life. Every few months, I get away to a nearby Benedictine abbey for twenty-four hours of silence and solitude. Afterwards, I am able to more fully enter into the lives of others with listening ears and an attentive heart. As we come alongside others, we are wise to learn to love silence, to become better listeners, and to offer words that bring healing, help, and refreshment.

91. Ibid., 123.
92. Psalm 141:3.
93. Gregory, *Pastoral Rule*, 124.
94. Ibid., 123.
95. James 1:19.

CHAPTER 36

The Lazy and the Hasty

Around three in the afternoon I regularly face an important life decision: nap or coffee. Sometimes I nod off for a short afternoon snooze. Fifteen minutes later, I'm refreshed and better prepared to finish my day of work with clarity and focus. Sometimes a cup of coffee or a brisk beach walk serves the same purpose: to wake up my mind and body.

There are some people who find it hard to get going each day, lacking basic motivation or purpose. There are others who find it hard to shut down, lacking the ability to sit still, get centered, or settle down. Either way, as we come alongside others, we are called to help people find their inner balance, avoiding the soul extremes of laziness and hastiness.

Those inclined to laziness lack zeal, and are frequently "overcome by a powerful, but hidden, sloth."[96] The words and phrases Gregory uses to describe this troubling state of the human soul include torpor, idleness, doing nothing, loss of vigilance, neglect for discipline, and slothfulness. "Laziness brings on deep sleep,"[97] warns Solomon the Wise, writing this and other ancient proverbs to awaken people from their spiritual slumber, a state of the soul prevalent among too many in our day just as then.

Gregory also cautions those inclined towards hastiness, those people who are in such a hurry they can "barely discern what is good," and "typically do not inspect the things they do but only afterwards realize that they ought not to have done them."[98] Again, Gregory refers to the wisdom of Solomon with the ancient proverb, "Let your eyes look directly forward, and your gaze be straight before you."[99] When we allow time to pause for our eyes to look ahead just a little, we take better steps and stumble less often. "The one who fails to look in front of him, through consideration of what he is about to do, advances with his eyes closed." Though hasty people continue on their journey, they do not see clearly where they are going, neglect to take time to listen to good counsel, and thus, often do not

96. Gregory, *Pastoral Rule*, 125.
97. Proverbs 19:15.
98. Gregory, *Pastoral Rule*, 127.
99. Proverbs 4:25.

know where best to place "the steps of [their] activity."[100] Better to wake up, discover anew God's good purpose for your life, take time to listen to good counsel from a soul mentor, and then with quiet confidence step forward into your day, fulfilling God's way of life: "to do justice, and to love kindness, and to walk humbly with your God."[101]

CHAPTER 37

The Meek and the Angry

This past winter, we planted over two hundred tulip bulbs in our front yard. That same day, we pruned back our rose bushes and trimmed up the garden in preparation for the coming of spring. A few months later, we had the daily delight of seeing new growth in our garden as tulips bloomed, offering beauty to our neighborhood.

Gregory loved the metaphor of the garden of the soul. "Being the great gardener . . . [God] waters some shoots, but others he prunes."[102] Gregory draws upon the writings of St. Paul for this picture of God as a gardener:

> I planted, Apollos watered, but God gave the growth. So neither the one who plants nor the one who waters is anything, but only God who gives the growth. The one who plants and the one who waters have a common purpose, and each will receive wages according to the labor of each. For we are God's servants, working together; you are God's field . . .[103]

As God's field, we are made to grow and be fruitful. God gives the growth. Yet some are hesitant to grow, while others grow in ways that are unfruitful. Those who are hesitant to grow are to be watered with encouragement, that they may overcome obstacles of idleness and inactivity, and press on in the good work of fruitful living.

100. Gregory, *Pastoral Rule*, 127.
101. Micah 6:8.
102. Gregory, *Pastoral Rule*, 129.
103. 1 Corinthians 3:6–9.

On the other hand, there are those who are quick to anger, jump to conclusions, rush into action before any consideration is given to the results, and are easily angered with the slow process of maturity. When such people are put into positions of leadership, "they confuse the lives of their subordinates and destroy the stillness of tranquility" with their impulsive anger and rage.[104] Some deceive themselves with their anger, thinking all anger is good, as though all fire is good. On the one hand, there is the holy fire of zeal which comes from the Spirit of God to light the fire of passion and purpose in the heart like lighting a wood stove. But there is also the unhealthy fire of resentment, malice, and rage, which loves burning bridges, hurting others, promoting strife, and leaving behind destruction. James wrote long ago about anger and meekness with these words:

> Let everyone be quick to listen, slow to speak, slow to anger; for your anger does not produce God's righteousness. Therefore rid yourselves of all sordidness and rank growth of wickedness, and welcome with meekness the implanted word that has the power to save your souls.[105]

When we come alongside another who is easily angered, "it is necessary that those who confront them do so not with anger, but with all possible calmness."[106] When trying to help someone rid himself of "rank growth," act as though you are pruning thorn bushes in a garden and work thoughtfully and calmly. When working to bring fruitfulness to an angry person, we must "put off our correction of them until after the commotion of their anger," and seek to win their respect with "a sort of careful respectfulness."[107] By God's goodness and grace, an angry person will welcome meekness, and a meek person will welcome newfound zeal. Springtime will come to both with new seedlings and signs of emerging fruitfulness.

104. Gregory, *Pastoral Rule*, 127.
105. James 1:19–21.
106. Gregory, *Pastoral Rule*, 130.
107. Ibid., 129.

CHAPTER 38

The Humble and the Arrogant

At six feet, four inches, I am considered by most people a tall man. I've often been asked to reach things on the top shelf or been employed as a human ladder by "height- disadvantaged" people. One of the hardest things for tall people, though, is to stoop down low to the ground.

These two movements of the body express similar movements of the soul: reaching high and stooping low. Both are part of what makes us unique among God's creatures. Along with all other animals, we have a physical body with earthly appetites for food, sex, drink, and sleep. Yet we also have a soul, with lofty desires for faith, hope. and love. We have the capacity to stoop low to the earth and to soar high among the stars. This same capacity can lead us into ways of living which are harmful to ourselves and to others, or into ones which bring life and goodness to ourselves and others. These two paths are the way of the humble and the way of the arrogant.

The longest chapter in *The Rule of St Benedict* is the chapter on humility.[108] In that chapter, Benedict describes humility as a ladder we set up in our lives, with twelve rungs or steps. Benedict writes, "If we want to reach the highest summit of humility, if we desire to attain speedily that exaltation in heaven to which we climb by the humility in this present life, then by our ascending actions we must set up that ladder." [109] Benedict offers twelve steps or rungs on this ladder of humility. I've paraphrased them as follows:

1) Put God first.

2) Imitate Christ.

3) Submit to God.

4) Patiently endure.

5) Confess.

6) Learn contentment.

108. RB 7.
109. RB 7.1, 5–6.

7) Stoop low.

8) Be accountable to others.

9) Learn to listen.

10) Laugh more.

11) Practice gentleness.

12) Live a life of humility.[110]

Benedict designed his twelve-step program for recovery from arrogance 1,500 years before Alcoholics Anonymous was created. As a monk, Gregory lived according to Benedict's writing, including living according to Benedict's twelve-step program of humility. Thus, it is not surprising that Gregory writes, "it should be said to the humble that whenever they lower themselves, they ascend to the likeness of God."[111] That is to say, we ascend by stooping. As Jesus declared, "all who exalt themselves will be humbled, but all who humble themselves will be exalted."[112]

Just as the humble love to stoop low to help others, the arrogant love to climb high to help themselves. Oxford professor C. S. Lewis wrote the following about pride:

> According to Christian teachers, the essential vice, the utmost evil, is Pride. Unchastity, anger, greed, drunkenness, and all that, are mere fleabites in comparison: it was through Pride that the devil became the devil: Pride leads to every other vice: it is the complete anti-God state of mind."[113]

One of the great dangers of pride or arrogance is that sometimes it will masquerade as false humility. Some arrogant people will let everyone know how much they don't deserve recognition or announce to anyone they meet how lowly they are. The odd thing about humility is that it doesn't make a show of itself. The humble are "down-to-earth" people. True humility is like good earth, humus, which receives rain, sun, and seed to grow good fruit.[114]

When coming alongside a person who is full of pride, Gregory wisely writes, "it will generally be easier to persuade [them] that amendment is

---

110. For a detailed study of Benedict's twelve steps of humility in light of Alcoholics Anonymous's twelve steps, see my previous book, Robinson, *Ancient Paths*, 28–39.

111. Gregory, *Pastoral Rule*, 132.

112. Luke 18:14.

113. Lewis, *Mere Christianity*, 96.

114. "Humility" is etymologically related to *humus,* or "good earth."

beneficial if we speak about their improvement as though it would help us rather than them."[115] Ask the arrogant if they wouldn't mind doing us a favor that would be for our good. Then ask them to stoop low and care for someone else's need besides their own. Gregory once again turns to the medical analogy to help us better understand this approach to the problem of arrogance. "The sweetness of honey is added to the bitterness of medicine, so that what is beneficial for health will not taste harsh or bitter. And as the taste is abated with sweetness, the deadly illness is expelled by the bitter medicine."[116] Then, with a liberal dose of praise, we may find the arrogant willing to accept a change of direction, and ascend by descending to bring health to others. In so doing, they may be surprised to find within themselves the growing gifts of life, joy, and inner health.

CHAPTER 39

The Stubborn and the Indecisive

When I was growing up, my family owned a sweet but stubborn donkey named Jemima. She loved eating oats, but refused to be led. She resisted anyone telling her what to do and would kick you if you dared step in her way. When we moved from California to Washington, we had to get her into the covered trailer. It was a battle of wills, human versus donkey. Only when gently coaxed with the sweetness of oats would Jemima finally give in, step up the ramp, and enter the trailer.

Similarly, there are some people who resist anyone telling them what to do. Gregory affectionately calls such people "the obstinate," those who "never yield to the advice of others."[117] Stubborn people are to be mentored in a different way than those who are uncertain about life, those who "in the indecisiveness of their thoughts fluctuate in their judgment from one

---

115. Gregory, *Pastoral Rule,* 133.
116. Ibid.
117. Ibid., 134.

moment to another."[118] The stubborn are not flexible enough. The indecisive are too flexible. Both have much to learn from one another.

In Gregory's view, stubborn people tend "to think themselves to be greater than they actually are," and are "being held captive by their pride." [119] With gentle coaxing and the "sweetness of oats," some stubborn people may be willing to be let out of their self-made prison, come to acknowledge "the haughtiness of their thoughts," and "study to correct their ways."[120] For them, a mentor should hold forth the sweetness of divine wisdom, pointing out the example of Christ, who declared, "I seek to do not my own will but the will of him who sent me . . . for I have come down from heaven, not to do my own will, but the will of him who sent me."[121]

In our time, just as when Gregory wrote his *Pastoral Care*, there are winds of change which buffet and bend us in many directions, including cultural, relational, philosophical, emotional, and spiritual forces. Those who are well-founded in their souls endure these winds, stabilized by the roots of their convictions, not changing with every passing fad or fancy that comes along. The indecisive are easily swayed or swept away by the "winds of mutability"[122] as Gregory calls these forces which beat upon the soul. Just as plants need a good root system, we need stability in our lives. When we disregard or undervalue our souls, we are too easily "tossed to and fro and blown about by every wind of doctrine, by people's trickery, by their craftiness . . ."[123] Better to strengthen our inner life by establishing the soul in God's wisdom, while increasing the flexibility of our inner life by empowering the soul in God's love.

118. Ibid.

119. Ibid., 134, 135.

120. Ibid., 135.

121. John 5:30; 6:38.

122. Gregory, *Pastoral Rule*, 134.

123. Ephesians 4:14.

CHAPTER 40

The Excessive and the Abstinent

According to the Centers for Disease Control and Prevention, "more than one-third of U.S. adults (35.7 percent) are obese. During the past twenty years, there has been a dramatic increase in obesity in the United States and rates remain high."[124] As a pastor, I was distressed to read that statistics for obesity among clergy may be even worse. "One study shows that seventy-six percent of clergy were either overweight or obese, compared to sixty-one percent of the general population."[125] Health troubles related to obesity include heart disease, hypertension, diabetes, stroke, and cancer, all of which are leading causes of preventable deaths. Obesity in America is one of many signs that we live in a culture of excess that causes widespread troubles for millions of people.

Though millions struggle with problems related to excess in the United States, millions of others in this country as well as around the world struggle daily with problems related to shortage, including lack of such basic needs as water, medicine, shelter, education, food, and parenting. Somehow, in the midst of this strange world of opposites, we seek the way of wisdom and balance, the way of moderation, compassion, and celebration.

Gregory's generation also struggled with problems related to self-indulgence and addiction. Gregory warns against "addiction to gluttony," claiming that "excessive speaking, laziness, and wanton lust accompany gluttony."[126] Those who lack self-control with food often struggle with excess in other areas of life as well, such as excess use of sleep, television, entertainment, or sex. Many also struggle with a lack of motivation, and have difficulty taking responsibility for personal wellness or slothful living.

While some love to feast, others love to fast. The abstinent also sometimes fall prey to self-indulgence through practices of self-denial, which can easily lead to self-pity or self-righteousness. "The sins of impatience and pride often accompany abstinence."[127] Those who curtail the desires

124. See http://www.cdc.gov/obesity/data/facts.html (accessed on July 1, 2014).
125. Burns, Chapman, and Guthrie, *Resilient Ministry*, 61.
126. Gregory, *Pastoral Rule*, 136.
127. Ibid.

of the body by practicing daily self-control may become impatient with those around them who indulge in bodily pleasures. One expression of abstinence may be found in a person's approach to fitness. There are some people who live to train, going to the gym daily, always heading out on a run, or constantly exercising their bodies to training DVDs. In their conversations, they love to discuss personal records, new diets, body mass index, marathons they are training for, or the latest running shoe designs. While physical fitness is an excellent goal for anyone, when it becomes our central life pursuit, it may also become a form of self-indulgence or addictive living.

In the realm of spirituality, there are some who equate holiness with self-denial, thinking themselves better than others because of what they give up, including sleep, sex, food, coffee, alcohol, and other physical attractions. As Scripture reminds us, various forms of abstinence may "have indeed an appearance of wisdom in promoting self-imposed piety, humility, and severe treatment of the body, but they are of no value in checking self-indulgence."[128] True spirituality is best revealed through love, including love of God, love of self, and love of others.

Therefore, let those who mortify the flesh "take care that the spirit of impatience not erupt. For there is no virtue in conquering the flesh if the spirit of wrath emerges."[129] On the other hand, there is also no virtue in indulging the flesh. Therefore, let the excessive listen to ancient wisdom: "Be on guard so that your hearts are not weighed down with dissipation and drunkenness and the worries of this life . . ."[130] Better to focus our lives upon loving God and learning to love others, including people in this world who daily live with hunger, lack of clean water, inadequate housing, lack of medicine, and lack of love. As the prophet Isaiah writes:

> Is not this the fast that I choose:
> to loose the bonds of injustice,
> to undo the thongs of the yoke,
> to let the oppressed go free,
> and to break every yoke?
> Is it not to share your bread with the hungry,
> and bring the homeless poor into your house;

128. Colossians 2:23.
129. Gregory, *Pastoral Rule*, 138.
130. Luke 21:34, quoted by Gregory in Part Three, chapter 19.

when you see the naked, to cover them,
and not to hide yourself from your own kin?[131]

Mentoring Inventory: First Half of Part Three

Halfway through Part Three of *Soul Mentoring*, I invite you to take some time to review Gregory's guidebook for Christian formation, considering ways you may deepen your life in Christ and develop greater wisdom for wise mentoring. The mentoring inventory below is drawn from the first half of Part Three of Gregory's *Pastoral Care*, asking you to consider three steps of self-examination.

Step One: For each of the twenty pairs in the first half of Part Three, mark an X along the continuum between each pair, identifying the place along this spectrum which most accurately describes your life and character. Go back through the first half of Part Three to review any pairs which may not be clear to you.

Step Two: For each of the twenty pairs below, mark a star along the spectrum between these opposites, identifying the place along the continuum where you'd like your life to grow in the future.

Step Three: Look over the twenty pairs and write in the space below any notes or impressions which come to mind as you review your life in light of these personality types and the potential growth for your life in the future.

1. Masculine--Feminine
2. Young--Old
3. Poor--Rich
4. Joyful---Sad
5. Leader---Follower
6. Employee---Employer
7. Educated---Uneducated
8. Bold---Shy
9. Assertive--Timid
10. Impatient---Patient

131. Isaiah 58:6–7.

11. Generous--Envious

12. Sincere---Insincere

13. Healthy---Sick

14. Sensitive--Hardened

15. Silent---Talkers

16. Lazy---Hasty

17. Meek--Angry

18. Humble---Arrogant

19. Stubborn--Indecisive

20. Excessive--Abstinent

CHAPTER 41

Givers and Takers

We are now halfway through Part Three of *Pastoral Care,* Gregory's catalogue of forty pairs of personality types. After completing the mentoring
inventory, you may find yourself identifying with one side against the other,
and growing weary of hearing about people on the other side. For mentees,
this ancient guidebook invites you to look beyond yourself into the life of
someone very different from yourself, and seek to live a more balanced life.
For mentors, Gregory keeps encouraging you to stretch yourself to learn to
discern the character of a mentee, caring for others in light of their unique
personalities rather than forcing them to fit into your framework. Written
into this book is an inherent humility, a willingness to step outside ourselves into the lives of others for the sake of nurturing growth of the soul.
We do this by wrestling with opposing forces within our lives.

Years ago, on a week-long service trip to Mexico, I bought a small
sculpture of two kings wrestling. One was upside down, in the clutches of
the one standing. Looking more closely at the two, you discovered the upside-down king was likely going to win the match. Such is the way of giving

and receiving. Whenever I've returned from a mission trip to Mexico, my life is turned upside down. I come home with a wrestling match in my heart and lifestyle. Part of me feels proud to have been so generous to give up a whole week to live among poor people, giving of my time, talent, and finances to help the needy. Another part of me realizes that the people in the very poor villages of other countries are truly richer than I am in their attitudes toward life, willing to share abundantly of their limited resources with joyful hearts.

Is it harder for you to give or to receive? Ask a person in their eighties and they will tell you that it is much harder to receive, especially when they've been giving to and serving others all their lives. When seniors finally come to a place where they are required to rely upon the kindness and service of others, it is hard for many of them to learn to receive. There are some people who naturally love to give. Others are naturally inclined to receiving. Often, these two opposites fall in love and get married, in part because they find someone who appreciates them but also has a gift they do not possess.

Some givers tend to elevate themselves above receivers, allowing pride "to swell in their minds" at the thought of their beneficence. Such givers may be encouraged to give "all the more humbly, in the knowledge that the things that they dispense are not their own." [132] Everyone receives good gifts given by God. As the poem by Matthias Claudius declares, "All good gifts around us are sent by heaven above." [133] In giving good gifts to others though, we are wise to discern our motives and seek to give in ways which best benefit the receiver. Gregory instructs givers with these words:

> They should not be too hasty and scatter their goods unprofitably, nor should they be too slow and torment their petitioners. Moreover, they should not allow the desire for receiving a favor in return emerge, otherwise the desire for transitory praise will extinguish the fire for giving. [134]

Wise motivation for giving is found in Paul's Second Letter to the Corinthians. "Each of you must give as you have made up your mind, not reluctantly or under compulsion, for God loves a cheerful giver." [135] The Greek

132. Gregory, *Pastoral Rule*, 141.

133. "We Plow the Fields, and Scatter" by Matthias Claudius (1782). See http://www.hymnary.org/text/we_plow_the_fields_and_ scatter (accessed on July 15, 2014).

134. Gregory, *Pastoral Rule*, 141.

135. 2 Corinthians 9:7.

word used in this sentence for cheerful, *hilaron,* is the root of our words "hilarity" and "hilarious." True giving arises out of a joyful heart, a playful heart overflowing with gratitude for all that has been given to us. The true measure of giving is not in the amount given, but the attitude of the heart in the act of giving.

On the other side of this divide, we find people who think mostly of themselves, who look out for number one, and who "are always looking to expand [their] own possessions at another's expense."[136] Gregory compares such a taker as "a captured bird, because as he looks greedily upon the bait of earthly things, he does not perceive that he steps into the noose of sin."[137] Gregory also realizes there are givers and takers, mentors and tormentors. A counselor I know has encouraged me to learn to view tormentors as mentors who are there to teach me important lessons I would not learn any other way, such as learning to look behind the outward expressions of anger or hostility to the inner life of a soul in pain. Jesus calls us to a life of love, including loving those who are unloving. "You have heard that it was said, 'You shall love your neighbor and hate your enemy.' But I say to you, Love your enemies and pray for those who persecute you, so that you may be children of your Father in heaven."[138] Wise mentors help such people discover the joy of giving gifts, including the gift of love to those who torment us. When selfish people realize they are truly loved, they may begin to recognize "the fleetingness of the present life,"[139] and begin to walk with others on soul paths of gratitude, forgiveness, and generosity.

CHAPTER 42

The Thrifty and the Wasteful

Jack Sprat and his wife may still be found wandering the frozen food section in your local supermarket. There are those who can eat no meat and

136. Gregory, *Pastoral Rule,* 144.
137. Ibid., 145.
138. Matthew 5:43–45.
139. Gregory, *Pastoral Rule,* 145.

others who can eat no lean. Some people love to save. Others love to spend. Mentoring the thrifty is a different work than mentoring the wasteful. The thrifty are to be advised to "learn carefully that the earth from which they come is common to all and produces nourishment for all in equal proportion."[140] Gregory's vision of the earth is rooted in the ancient Judeo-Christian world view which proclaims, "The earth is the Lord's and all that is in it, the world, and those who live in it."[141] We are all stewards of this earth. We belong to God. The earth also belongs to God. As stewards, we learn to be generous with God's provisions, to creatively find ways to care for others, especially out of the abundance of what's been given to us. As Gregory warns, "Therefore, it is foolish for [the thrifty] to suppose themselves innocent who proclaim that the common gift of God belongs to their own private stocks."[142]

Privatization is a common way of life among twenty-first-century people in the West. Millions of us have our own private homes, and private bank accounts protected with multiple firewalls, passwords, locked doors, and security cameras. I'm a homeowner, have bank accounts, and take a variety of private approaches to daily living. Those who look with their hearts seek in others a heart of mercy and justice, encouraging people to use stuff more often for the common good. Gregory mentors the thrifty to be encouraged to "bear the fruit of good works," and warns against living selfish, private lives apart from the needy of this world. Those who want to save more and more are to be encouraged to "put away the sluggishness of improvident security," lest they be "cut off from the present life, as if from the life of the roots."[143] Only when a person's life is well-rooted in the love and justice of God will they generously offer their lives to benefit others.

On the other hand, the wasteful include people who are wasteful with the gifts God has given them, those who borrow from lenders to get more of what they want, and those who love to be recognized by others "for their external show of goodness," making a big thing out of their generosity.[144] Mentoring the wasteful requires training a person in the spiritual art of stewardship. "Such persons must first be admonished to learn how to

140. Ibid., 146.
141. Psalm 24:1.
142. Gregory, *Pastoral Rule*, 146.
143. Ibid., 147.
144. Ibid.

retain, within reason, some of their possessions."[145] Teaching people how to save, how to faithfully steward God's gifts, and how to prepare for the future through responsible fiscal decision-making is a neglected aspect of soul mentoring. Our finances often express outwardly what is in our hearts. As Jesus taught, "For where your treasure is, there your heart will be also."[146]

Today, the wasteful often buy on credit what they don't need, and find themselves impoverished through lack of discipline or financial responsibility. The average credit card debt in the United States in 2014 is $15,000 per person; the average mortgage debt is $150,000; and the average student loan debt in the United States is $33,000.[147] In total, American consumers are nearly twelve trillion dollars in debt, with over $850 billion in credit card debt alone. These numbers are up from 2013. As a consumer society, we love buying on credit, borrowing from banks and lenders the funds to use money we don't have to get more stuff we often don't need. As the prophet Haggai warned thousands of years ago, the wasteful are like people who "have sown much, and harvested little; you eat, but you never have enough; you drink, but you never have your fill; you clothe yourselves, but no one is warm; and you that earn wages earn wages to put them into a bag with holes."[148]

Better to mentor people in the ancient art of giving, helping them discover the joy of generosity and caring for others through acts of kindness, including donations to help the needy. As Thornton Wilder tells us in his 1955 hit play *The Matchmaker* through the voice of Dolly Levi, "Money, pardon the expression, is like manure. It's not worth a thing unless it's spread around encouraging young things to grow."[149]

145. Ibid., 148.

146. Matthew 6:21.

147. See http://www.nerdwallet.com/blog/credit-card-data/average-credit-card-debt -household/ (accessed on July 9, 2014).

148. Gregory, *Pastoral Rule*, 149. Gregory quotes from Haggai 1:6.

149. http://www.thorntonwilder.com/hello-dolly.html (accessed on July 9, 2014).

CHAPTER 43

The Quarrelers and the Peaceable

Many years ago, I came upon an older man punching a college student in the face in a public place. Without thinking, I stepped between them, grabbed the older man's wrists and tried to stop the fight. Of course, the older man turned his wrath away from his college-aged son and focused all his red-faced anger on me, yelling at me and even hitting me a few times. Finally, he walked away in disgust once he realized with embarrassment that many others were watching his outrageous behavior.

We are a warring species. A soul at war within will inevitably lead to conflict with other humans. There are people who have hearts full of anger, envy, or arrogance. What lies at the heart of war? Where do conflicts and quarrels come from? St. James writes,

> Do they not come from your cravings that are at war within you? You want something and do not have it; so you commit murder. And you covet something and cannot obtain it; so you engage in disputes and conflicts. You do not have, because you do not ask. You ask and do not receive, because you ask wrongly, in order to spend what you get on your pleasures.[150]

Soul mentoring reaches into that place of the human heart, and attempts to guide a person to find inner healing and restoration in the inner war zone. St. James reveals the two types of fruit which often grow in the human soul.

> For where there is envy and selfish ambition, there will also be disorder and wickedness of every kind. But the wisdom from above is first pure, then peaceable, gentle, willing to yield, full of mercy and good fruits, without a trace of partiality or hypocrisy. And a harvest of righteousness is sown in peace for those who make peace.[151]

In place of bitter envy, a person can learn contentment by receiving the gentle and peaceable gift of "wisdom from above." In the place of selfish ambition, a person may discover the willingness to yield and the good fruit

---

150. James 4:1–3.
151. James 3:16–18.

of serving others. Gregory challenges his readers to "strive to keep the unity of the Spirit in the bond of peace . . . even as you are called in one hope of your calling."[152] Gregory continues, "The 'one hope of your calling,' therefore, is not achieved if we do not strive for it with a mind in unity with our neighbor."[153] Practically, a person may speak in favor of world peace, yet struggle to live in peace with his neighbors or with members of her own family. Peacemaking involves learning to live peaceably with people we meet daily, including angry, critical, cynical, or conflictive people. Mentoring quarrelsome people calls us to hold up a mirror that a mentee may see the conflict within their own heart, discover the gift of forgiveness and reconciliation, and begin to learn to live in unity with others. This is easier to write about than it is to practice. I believe such a way of life becomes possible when we first allow our souls to be overcome by God's amazing love.

There are others who "love the peace that they have too excessively."[154] As a middle child, I learned to keep the peace by acting like a clown within my family, trying to get people to laugh in the midst of conflict. To this day I avoid conflict, and do harm to myself and others by excessively loving the peace that I have rather than facing conflict. Gregory warns us against false forms of peace, such as silencing our criticism of others when they engage in unhealthy ways of living, in order to "hold peace with them."[155] Many marriages would be better served if husbands and wives gave one another permission to open their hearts and mouths, to humbly listen to one another, and seek to build a deeper, more lasting, and peaceful marriage by working through the difficulties and conflicts rather than trying to live with the pretense of peace.

Most married couples would also benefit from a marriage mentor couple as well as professional marriage counseling to accomplish this miracle of growth in the face of conflict.[156] Gregory says we shouldn't "fear to disturb the temporal peace by offering words of correction."[157] In a world overwhelmed by conflict and war, including the domestic world of marriage, when my soul grows weary and anxious with my own inner troubles and external conflicts, I often return to nature to be renewed. When I am

152. Gregory quotes from St. Paul in Ephesians 4:3–4.

153. Gregory, *Pastoral Rule*, 149.

154. Ibid., 151.

155. Ibid., 152.

156. See Drs. Les and Leslie Parrott, *The Complete Guide to Marriage Mentoring*.

157. Gregory, *Pastoral Rule*, 153.

stressed, weary, or fresh out of hope, along with Kentucky farmer-poet Wendell Berry, I return to God's creation to find restoration for my soul as I "come into the peace of wild things."[158]

CHAPTER 44

Sowers of Discord and Sowers of Peace

The Dalai Lama often speaks of world peace and calls his listeners to live lives of peace. "Everybody loves to talk about calmness and peace, whether in a family, national, or international context, but without inner peace how can we make real peace? World peace through hatred and force is impossible."[159] Gregory would agree completely. "It is the well ordering of the internal [soul] that keeps the external members in order."[160] Gregory describes this inner work of peacemaking as an act of gardening, including pulling weeds, sowing good seeds, and rooting our lives in love.

Daily we are planting seeds of discord or seeds of peace in the lives of others. Usually, we do not realize what we've done, either for good or for ill. Yet our lives are making a difference, for better or for worse. Gregory calls mentors to help people become more aware of the seeds they sow and to seek to be sowers of peace rather than sowers of discord. How is this possible? Mentors help mentees with the condition of the soil of their soul. In Jesus's classic parable, he portrays the soul as containing four kinds of soil, including hard dirt, rocky ground, thorny land, and good soil. In my experience, most people are a mixture of soil types, with part of our soul unreceptive to the good seeds being sown in our lives, part of our soul clogged or choked with other forces, while, at the same time, other parts of our inner life are good earth ready to bear fruit.

The "fruit of good works," according to Gregory, will "spring from the unity of charity." On the contrary, sowers of strife, who "separate

---

158. Berry, *New Collected Poems*, 79.

159. Gee, *Words of Wisdom*, 19.

160. Gregory, *Pastoral Rule*, 154.

themselves, through discord, from the lifeline of love will wither and die."[161] By failing to tend to the garden of the soul, a person allows seeds of strife to be sown within. Such a person will end up sowing strife themselves among others, and "by sowing strife, they extinguish charity, which is the mother of all the virtues."[162] Wise mentoring involves instilling "a love for internal peace" among those we mentor, "for only then will they be able to enjoy the benefits of external peace."

We are invited to actively bring peace to our world, person to person, in each encounter we experience with others. This is not easily done, for not everything depends on us. As St. Paul writes, "If it is possible, so far as it depends on you, live peaceably with all."[163] What depends on us? Cultivating our inner life of peace is a choice each of us can make, living inwardly in peace before stepping out our front door into our discordant world. At the root of this way of life is what Thomas Merton calls the "problem of love."

> The whole problem of our time is the problem of love: how are we going to recover the ability to love ourselves and to love one another? The reason why we hate one another and fear one another is that we secretly or openly hate and fear our own selves. And we hate ourselves because the depths of our being are a chaos of frustration and spiritual misery. Lonely and helpless, we cannot be at peace with others because we are not at peace with ourselves, and we cannot be at peace with ourselves because we are not at peace with God.[164]

CHAPTER 45

The Ignorant and the Proud

Picture an oil lamp sitting on a wooden table in a bedroom as a mother cares for a sick child in the middle of the night. Gregory frequently writes

161. Ibid.
162. Ibid., 155.
163. Romans 12:18.
164. Merton, *The Living Bread*, xii–xiii.

in pictures, describing the ancient wisdom of sacred Scripture as "a type of lantern for us in the night of this present life," or as "medicine to the sick."[165] There are some who live in the darkness of ignorance, who refuse to light the lamp of their mind and heart by the light of sacred Scripture. They may have a Bible and may have opened and read from this book, but have failed to understand the writings—like someone who has gone into the attic to read, but failed to turn on the attic light. When we read in the dark, our minds fail to perceive the wonders and splendors of what is written. When we mentor in the dark, our hearts fail to perceive the wonders and splendors of what lies hidden in the soul until the lantern of wisdom shines upon the "night of this present life." In this darkness, people remain in their sickness without wise soul physicians to bring them the medicine that restores inner health.

As written in Part One, some mentors hastily rush into mentoring without adequate training, despising "to follow another to a better understanding," and instead "[creating] for themselves an image of expertise among the uninformed masses."[166] In our day and age, anyone can go online and print off a certificate declaring their life fit for service, licensed to practice, credentialed to teach or mentor others. I once knew a minister who obtained his doctoral degree through an online course. After a few weeks of online studies, this fellow printed off his doctoral degree, and seriously began calling himself Doctor Hansen,[167] as though he had attained some lofty summit of wisdom, when all he had arrived at was a mere image of expertise. Such mentors are like the blind leading the blind, as the Teacher warns, "Can a blind person guide a blind person? Will not both fall into a pit?"[168]

Like my colleague Dr. Hansen, there are some who brashly enter into mentoring without ever being mentored themselves. They may have plenty of head knowledge but very little heart wisdom. Gregory encourages such people to "first examine themselves," to take time to explore our own weaknesses, shortcomings, and limitations that we may better care for other people with compassion. Gregory compares such a person to a "poor and unskilled physician who attempts to heal others but is not able to diagnose

---

165. Gregory, *Pastoral Rule*, 157.

166. Ibid.

167. Name changed by the author.

168. Luke 6:39.

SOUL MENTORING: PART THREE

his own wounds."[169] True wisdom is found when our "manner of speaking is consistent with the excellence of what is being said," and when what we say with words is also lived out with actions.[170] Solomon wrote long ago, "Drink water from your own cistern, flowing water from your own well."[171] We drink from our own cistern when we examine our inner life and consider in depth whether we are practicing what we preach. We drink "flowing water from [our] own well," when we are "nourished by the watering of [our] own words."[172] Whether ignorant or proud, we are all wise to return again and again to the well of ancient wisdom found in sacred Scripture, to drink deeply, filling our inner life with "flowing water" that we may bring refreshment and integrity to others, as the psalmist writes:

> They feast on the abundance of your house,
> and you give them drink from the river of your delights.
> For with you is the fountain of life;
> in your light we see light.[173]

CHAPTER 46

The Hesitant and the Hasty

In the previous chapter, we considered those who rush into mentoring without adequate preparation. Gregory follows this with words of encouragement for the hesitant and the hasty. There are some who are hesitant to mentor others either in word or deed. There are others who are hasty to speak and hasty to act. Both types of people need the guidance of wise soul mentors to guide them towards a more balanced way of living.

---

169. Gregory, *Pastoral Rule*, 159.
170. Ibid.
171. Proverbs 5:15, as quoted from Gregory, *Pastoral Rule*, 159.
172. Gregory, *Pastoral Rule*, 159.
173. Psalm 36:8–9.

96

There are some who would be excellent mentors, "but refuse because of an immoderate measure of humility."[174] While humility is an essential virtue for wise mentoring, there are some who hesitate to exercise their talents because they do not feel worthy, or they do not have sufficient self-confidence to speak to others with wisdom. There are some who indulge themselves in false humility, wallowing in their lack of self-worth, excessively focusing on themselves by telling others they are nothing and deserve nothing. Instead of putting their unique talents and gifts to use for the benefit of others, they hide behind walls of false humility, claiming they are not fit to serve others. Gregory compares such people to a doctor who denies "the medicine of life to dying souls," and to someone who "does not offer the bread of grace to those who are dying spiritually from a famine of the divine Word."[175]

Gregory points us to one of Jesus's famous parables, the parable of the Talents, in which an employer entrusts huge sums of money to his employees. To one he gives five talents, to another two, and to another one, "each according to his ability."[176] The first two servants take significant risks in investing their sums, making as much again as they were given. The first two employees doubled the amounts they were given, and thus received their employer's commendation. But the employee who was give one talent hides the amount, saying later to his employer, "I was afraid, and I went and hid your talent in the ground. Here you have what is yours."[177] God has given everyone gifts, "according to our ability." Some invest their gifts creatively, and end up multiplying what they've been given. Others, out of fear, hide their God-given gifts and talents, hesitant to invest their lives in service to others to multiply what they've been given. For them, even the little they've been given will ultimately be taken away. Let them hear the wisdom of David who wrote,

> I have not hidden your saving help within my heart,
> I have spoken of your faithfulness and your salvation;
> I have not concealed your steadfast love and your faithfulness
> from the great congregation.[178]

---

174. Gregory, *Pastoral Rule,* 160.

175. Ibid., 161.

176. Matthew 25:15. A "talent" is worth about twenty years of income.

177. Matthew 25:25.

178. Psalm 40:10; quoted in Gregory, *Pastoral Rule,* Part Three, chapter 25.

On the other side of the room we meet the hasty, who are quick to speak and quick to act. We must not be too quick to judge the hasty, for we live in a world that is intoxicated with speed. The digital revolution has radically changed the way we think about speed. We type a few words into a search engine, sending that signal through the freeway of the internet, bouncing signals off satellites, and up pops what we want, need, or desire within fractions of seconds. Some people get caught up in this vision of life, and see themselves as extensions of their tablet or smartphone, able to spit out instant answers to any question, with the world literally at their fingertips.

A friend recently told me a story of a fledgling crow he discovered on the ground in his backyard under a stand of evergreen trees. This juvenile was too hasty to leave its nest before it was ready to fly. Since he knew his neighbor's cat loved eating birds, my friend brought this young crow to the safety of his back deck. The parents were never far off, making a ruckus every time my friend came outside to feed it until it, was able to fly off on its own a few days later. Gregory warns against being overly hasty, telling us not to "seize prematurely what they are not able to do," and comparing such hasty people to young birds who "try to fly before their wings are fully developed," with the expected result of falling "from the height that they sought."[179]

Gregory also warns the hasty to consider "that if women give birth to children that are not fully formed, they fill not homes, but tombs."[180] Wise mentors help the hasty to learn to wait, to allow time for gestation and growth of our wings so that we may fly. We can learn well from the life of Jesus, who was willing to be taught and who "did not wish to become a teacher of men until his thirtieth year on earth." He also told his followers to "stay here in the city until you have been clothed with power from on high."[181] Sometimes, we prepare best by remaining still, resting, and attentively waiting. As John Milton wrote in his famous sonnet after he went blind, "They also serve who only stand and wait."[182]

179. Gregory, *Pastoral Rule*, 164.
180. Ibid.
181. Ibid.; see also Luke 24:49.
182. Hughes, *John Milton Complete*, 168.

CHAPTER 47

The First and the Last

One of the awkward moments of childhood is when teams are chosen on the playground. Two children step forward as captains to decide the fate of the other children, with some chosen first and others chosen last. Kids that are not chosen first may experience feelings of fear and embarrassment of being chosen last. These childhood fears are realized year after year and well into adulthood in many other settings, as either successes or failures come our way, bringing hopes and fears to life.

Gregory encourages mentors to advise "those who are successful in worldly pursuits" differently than "those who desire the things of the world but are worn out by the toil of adversity."[183] In our world today, the gap continues to widen between the haves and the have-nots. Those who prosper and those who struggle in "the toil of adversity" look at life differently and have valuable lessons to learn from one another.

When I've led short-term service projects among the poor, both in the United States and in Mexico, I've always been struck by the generosity and gratitude of people who have so little in the way of material success. One very poor Mexican woman brought our group of twenty a basketful of homemade tamales for our dinner. As we ate them that evening, our project leader told us the tamale dinner we were eating had cost the woman the equivalent of a week's earnings, a huge sacrifice for her, but was given with gratitude for our presence and help in her community. She was thankful that wealthy people from the United States had come to share God's love with her poor village. She seemed to me a person with true wealth.

The successful can easily lose sight of "the clarity of the sun" when we focus too much on "the dim light of the moon."[184] Gregory encourages us to view the dimness of earthly pursuits in light of the brilliance of heavenly pursuits. In the same paragraph, Gregory warns the wealthy about focusing too much on the gifts and neglecting the Giver, lest they "love their

---

183. Gregory, *Pastoral Rule*, 165.
184. Ibid.

pilgrimage more than their homeland."[185] We live in a state of exile in this life, traveling as pilgrims along our earthly journey. We are wise to travel light, with gratitude upon our hearts for the gift of life. "May the things that are provided to us be of service outwardly," Gregory asserts, "to the extent that they do not distract our souls from a desire for supernal delight."[186] When we are provided for in abundance, perhaps it is that we may help others live better lives through our "response of good works."

Those who struggle in this life, who stand at the back of the line, who are chosen last, have more opportunities to see how fleeting and temporary the rewards of this life really are. They are to be encouraged to consider how easily the prosperous fall into the "trap of sin," as Gregory describes the dangers and lures of wealth and material possessions. When we take our eyes off the treasures of this world and begin to live in light of eternity, true riches such as gratitude, compassion, and love begin to flourish within our souls. Jesus offered words of encouragement to those who struggle, declaring, "Blessed are the poor in spirit, for theirs is the kingdom of heaven."[187] One Albanian woman who took this teaching to heart changed the face of the twentieth century with her way of living among the poorest of the poor. Mother Teresa of Calcutta understood from years of working and living among the poor in India what they have to teach us, which she spoke of in her Nobel Peace Prize acceptance lecture in December, 1979.

> The poor people are very great people. They can teach us so many beautiful things. The other day one of them came to thank and said: You people who have vowed chastity you are the best people to teach us family planning. Because it is nothing more than self-control out of love for each other. And I think they said a beautiful sentence. And these are people who maybe have nothing to eat, maybe they have not a home where to live, but they are great people. The poor are very wonderful people.[188]

185. Ibid.

186. Ibid., 166.

187. Matthew 5:3.

188. Mother Teresa of Calcutta, from her Nobel Peace Lecture, December 11, 1979; see http://www.nobelprize.org/nobel_prizes/peace/laureates/1979/teresa-lecture.html (accessed on July 1, 2014).

CHAPTER 48

The Married and the Single

At the time of this writing, my wife and I have been married for thirty-four years. Before getting married, I was single for twenty-four years. Both ways of life have their joys and challenges. One of the wisest words of wisdom we received before we were married was to minimize the number of external changes during our first year of marriage to better focus upon the internal changes that marriage brings. Of course, we didn't follow this advice. Instead, in our first twelve months of marriage, we moved twice, I began a new career, we had our first baby, and we experienced the death of a parent and a grandparent. On the Holmes and Rahe stress scale, a list of forty-three life events that cause stress which can contribute to illness, our score easily surpassed the 300 mark, pushing well into the danger zone, and thus we had a "very high risk of becoming ill in the near future."[189]

Marital status is another significant factor in mentoring, both for mentors and mentees. As Gregory writes, "those who are bound by wedlock and those who are free of the ties of marriage should be advised differently."[190] Healthy marriages do not happen by chance but by intention, "as they mutually consider what is good for their partner."[191] What is good for married couples? Help couples seek in their life together the highest good for one another, and so live their married life "in this world without relinquishing their desire for God."[192] Along with many other ancient writers, Gregory elevates singleness and celibacy as a higher calling than marriage. Gregory also believed that marital intercourse was only intended "for the purpose of producing children." Though many writers from Gregory's period of church history viewed marital sex as limited to procreation, the Bible clearly teaches that God created us as sexual beings, and Scripture celebrates sexual relations within the marriage of one man and one woman as very

189. See Thomas H. Holmes and Richard H. Rahe, "The Social Readjustment Rating Scale," *Journal of Psychosomatic Research* 11, no. 2 (August 1967) 213–218. See http://www.mindtools.com/pages/article/newTCS_82.htm (accessed on July 1, 2014).

190. Gregory, *Pastoral Rule*, 169.

191. Ibid.,

192. Ibid.

good, not just for procreation but also as an expression of God's creative goodness. The Bible teaches that both marriage and singleness are gifts and callings from God. The healthiest marriages I've known have been deeply rooted in eternity while living faithfully and fully here on earth; as Gregory writes, they "rejoice in the present good" while continuing to "link their hope (with every consolation) to the everlasting good."[193]

Those who are single are to be encouraged not to be overcome with temporal anxieties and ambitions, but to be "free and all the more able to do greater things," such as devoting their lives to loving God and caring for others.[194] Of course, the Bible warns both married and single people against sexual immorality, calling us all to take the high road of purity and fidelity in our sexual life, whether single or married. When singles continually "suffer from the storms of temptation," according to Gregory, they "should seek the port of marriage."[195] After thirty-four years of marriage, I love Gregory's picture of marriage as a haven from storms, but know from experience that God also calls married couples out across deep waters to face storms and trials together.

Through decades of married life, or across the years of celibate singleness, people awake with hope, lift their sails, and brave the waves of another day, as sung in the 1907 hymn "I Feel the Winds of God Today":

> I feel the winds of God today; today my sail I lift,
> Though heavy, oft with drenching spray, and torn with many a rift;
> If hope but light the water's crest, and Christ my bark will use,
> I'll seek the seas at His behest, and brave another cruise.[196]

---

193. Ibid.
194. Ibid., 173.
195. Ibid., 174.
196. Hymn lyrics by Jessie Adams, 1907; *Hymns for the Living Church*, 449.

CHAPTER 49

Sinners and Saints

Except in New Orleans, saints seem to be in short supply in our world today. Secular society balks at the ancient categories of saint and sinner, doubting they have anything to say about life in the twenty-first century. Blinded by the bright lights of celebrity scandals on the covers of tabloid news, we easily overlook the everyday holiness of ordinary saints standing next to us in the supermarket checkout line. Perhaps now is a good time to once again see ourselves and others as hybrid saints and sinners.

The phrase Martin Luther used to describe such amphibious living is *simul justus et peccator*, "simultaneously saint and sinner." Luther believed all people are broken and damaged in one way or another. We have all fallen short of God's glory, and continue throughout our life to stumble and fall short of God's glory until our dying breath. Luther also believed we are made right with God through faith in Jesus Christ as a gift from God. We are continually reunited to God by grace through faith, and accepted by God as beloved children until our dying breath.

Gregory loved the metaphor of sailing to describe the human condition, comparing us to survivors who have "suffered a shipwreck."[197] Part of our life's work is to "repair what has been damaged."[198] When seeking a mentor, we look for someone who has wisdom and experience in restoring and rebuilding areas of our life which have been damaged by our life voyage. Some of this damage comes to us from others who harm us and from life circumstances. Other damage we bring upon ourselves with dumb decisions, self-indulgent living, or immaturity. Whatever the cause, all people have some form of brokenness, hurt, or inner damage which needs healing grace. The best way to find this healing is by returning home "to the Lord, who welcomes us."[199] God does not hold our brokenness against us, but "expands the bosom of mercy to the one who returns," taking delight in all who come back to their heart's true home.[200]

197. Gregory, *Pastoral Rule*, 174.
198. Ibid.
199. Ibid., 176.
200. Ibid.

All people are created in God's image, imprinted with original goodness, beauty, and love. Part of the unique work of mentoring involves helping mentees "preserve intact the natural goodness that they received."[201] There are some people who live in simplicity and purity of heart, uncorrupted by the many temptations and diversions of this world, but always pursuing what is higher. "Since they stand at a high point," Gregory warns, "they should be advised that they remain aware that the more prominent place is where they stand, the more frequent will be the arrows of the one who lies in wait for us."[202]

One such high place is the life calling of celibacy. In our world today, celibate people are viewed as oddballs who likely have a problem. Over the years, I've had the privilege of getting to know monks through regular retreats to monasteries. The monks I've known have presented to me a sane, well-balanced, even playful view of life and intimacy. They have not "exalted vainly in their celibacy" as Gregory warns saints, but have focused their energies on loving God and loving others with amazing depth, humor, and compassion. Some entered the monastery out of brokenness, as though coming home. Gregory tells of such people: "The life that grows ardently in love for God after sin is more pleasing than innocence that grows lazy in its security."[203] One of the stories I love about St. Francis reveals his humility and humor. As Francis was entering a village on one of his travels across Italy, locals were bowing down before him, venerating him as a great saint. Francis was known to say, "Don't call me a saint, I could still go off and father a child."[204] We have within our souls, until our dying breath, both sinner and saint, with both a propensity to fall back gravely to earth while we continually aspire to rise to the glories of heaven.

201. Ibid., 174.

202. Ibid., 176–177.

203. Ibid., 178.

204. Quoted from http://www.friar.org/fileadmin/user_upload/StFrancis.pdf (accessed on July 1, 2014).

CHAPTER 50

Active and Contemplative

Martha loved to be active. Mary loved to sit still and listen. They lived in the same home as sisters. When Jesus came into their home, bringing the whole crew of men along with him, Martha got busy making the meal, a dinner for more than a dozen people requiring several hours of labor. Mary sat sill at the feet of Jesus, listening to his teaching, surrounded by men. Martha got upset at her sister, and was distracted by her many tasks. Jesus gently challenged Martha, saying "Martha, Martha, you are worried and distracted by many things; there is need of only one thing. Mary has chosen the better part, which will not be taken away from her." [205]

Gregory loved this story as a model for wholeness in the spiritual life. Personally, he was deeply drawn to the life of Mary, and loved the contemplative way of living. Vocationally, Gregory was called into the way of Martha, when he was elected as pope. These two sisters reveal two ways of living: the active way and the contemplative way. Some people live mostly in their head and heart; others live mostly in their bodies and actions. Contemplatives pursue careers involving head and heart, such as teaching, prayer, or counseling. Active people pursue careers involving movement and the body, such as construction, nursing, or athletics. Yet all people fall apart at one time or another. Contemplatives fall apart differently than the active. We all lose our way at times. Those who live mostly in their heads get lost in different ways than those who live mostly in their bodies. Transgressions of the body differ from transgressions of the mind. Failures of the mind differ from failures of the body. But we are wise to remember, as written in the previous chapter, that "all have sinned and fall short of the glory of God." [206]

Consider steps people take down stairs into the dark cellar of temptation, including temptations of thought and action. The first step into this dark place occurs when we flirt with temptation in our thoughts. Most often, our thought life is the starting point. We see something that sparks

205. Luke 10:41–42.
206. Romans 3:23.

fleeting thoughts of temptation. We consider what it would be like to have it. We toy with the idea long before holding the actual toy in our hands. Daily, our minds are bombarded with passing fancies and thoughts. The ancient art of soul mentoring calls us to help others begin to learn to train their minds to think well, and focus upon those thoughts which are healthy, loving, and true. As Paul wrote, "Finally, beloved, whatever is true, whatever is honorable, whatever is just, whatever is pure, whatever is pleasing, whatever is commendable, if there is any excellence and if there is anything worthy of praise, think about these things."[207]

We take the second step down into trouble when we consent to temptation, willfully choosing to go against what we know is best for us. As Gregory writes, "those who despise sins of thought should be advised to consider whether they have sinned only in their minds or if they have also sinned by consent."[208] Obviously, to entertain fleeting thoughts by giving consent to what previously was merely a passing fancy or desire, we step further down into the darkness of temptation. Martin Luther playfully remarked, "You cannot keep birds from flying over your head, but you can keep them from building a nest in your hair."[209]

We take a third step when our bodily desires give in to temptation. Our bodily desires for food, drink, sleep, comfort, power, and sex are strong motivators that may force us against our better judgment to enter into unhealthy actions of temptation. When we give in to temptation we pursue ways of living which stand in violation of our higher thoughts, values, and intentions. As Jesus taught the night of his temptation in the garden of Gethsemane, "the spirit indeed is willing, but the flesh is weak."[210] We give in to temptation because it looks good and feels good. The original temptation is described this way:

> So when the woman saw that the tree was good for food, and that it was a delight to the eyes, and that the tree was to be desired to make one wise, she took of its fruit and ate; and she also gave some to her husband, who was with her, and he ate. [211]

---

207. Philippians 4:8.

208. Gregory, *Pastoral Rule*, 181.

209. Quoted from Warren, *Purpose Driven Life*, 205.

210. Matthew 26:41.

211. Genesis 3:6.

First man and first woman gave in to temptation because the fruit of temptation seemed good for food, it was a delight to the eyes, and was desirable to the man and woman.

A fourth step away from the light of life is when we actively enter into a life of temptation by pursuing ways of corruption and darkness. Habits are formed intentionally over time. Both good habits and bad habits take time to develop. Corrupt ways of life are intentionally chosen by actively entering into a lifestyle of temptation, when we choose ways of darkness over and over until they are internalized. St. James gives us the progression: "One is tempted by one's own desire, being lured and enticed by it; then, when that desire has conceived, it gives birth to sin, and that sin, when it is fully grown, gives birth to death."[212]

Reverse these steps, and a person is able to journey back towards the light. Whether a person has stumbled down these steps in their thoughts or intentionally walked down this way through their choices and actions, all people may be restored, cleansed, and brought back upward into the light of love. First, we need to admit that we need help. Whether in our thoughts or actions, we all need help. Since temptations normally begin in our thought life, Gregory advises, "[sins] of thought are more easily forgiven because they have not developed into a completed action."[213] We will find it much easier to pull weeds when they first appear in our thoughts, rather than wait until they've taken root in our lifestyle.

Second, we remember our failures in our thoughts as well as in our actions, and choose to bring them before our eyes one by one.[214] "Therefore," encourages Gregory, "they are to be advised to consider individually each of their past transgressions, and while they bewail these defilements one by one, they can at the same time cleanse themselves entirely through their tears."[215]

Third, as we confess to God and to others the darkened state of our lives, by God's help we can truly be cleansed in body, mind, and soul. "For indeed," Gregory writes, "the mind does not grieve over different things in

---

212. James 1:14–15.

213. Gregory, *Pastoral Rule*, 182.

214. Ibid., 180. Gregory writes, "They should be advised to recall their sins before their eyes constantly."

215. Ibid.

the same way, but when it is more sharply pricked by this sin or that one, being in effect moved by them differently, it is purged of all of them."[216]

Finally, we are wise to seek help from others. Both "Marys" and "Marthas" need help from one another to learn to live in wholeness. Mary needs Martha. Martha needs Mary. Both need the healing word and action of Jesus. We cannot overcome ways of destruction alone. We are meant to be with others, living a life of love with God and others in our thoughts and in our actions, as we sit together at the feet of Jesus, and as we walk and work together into the light.

CHAPTER 51

Addiction and Codependence

Like a dog that returns to its vomit
is a fool who reverts to his folly.
The sow is washed only to wallow in the mud.[217]

Most who are reading this right now are struggling with some form of addiction. Many are struggling with codependence. We have all played the fool at times. We all need help out of the mud. According to psychiatrist Gerald May in his book *Addiction and Grace*, "We are all addicts in every sense of the word. Moreover, our addictions are our own worst enemies."[218] Though we may not wrestle with chemical dependence, all of us are attached in unhealthy ways to something, including such things as "ideas, work, relationships, power, moods, fantasies, and an endless variety of other things."[219] For those who are closely related to addicts, patterns of codependence, or "relationship addiction," can be equally unhealthy and destructive.[220] Codependents often live with one or more of the following

216. Ibid.
217. Proverbs 26:11 and 2 Peter 2:22.
218. May, *Addiction and Grace*, 3–4.
219. Ibid., 3.
220. For more information on codependency, see http://www.mentalhealthamerica.

symptoms: low self-esteem, excessive need for approval, a fear of abandonment, poor boundaries, problems with intimacy, obsessive behaviors, and denial they have a problem.[221]

What truly matters in such weighty areas of human life is how willing we are to seek the help of a mentor. Those who fall into the mud are wise to take a bath. Gregory astutely writes,

> The one who neglects to be clean after washing is the one who does not possess the innocence of his life after his tears. Therefore, they are washed but not clean who does not cease to bewail their actions but [still] continue to commit them.[222]

The trouble lies in the heart, with our motives. Until we come to the place where we admit we are powerless over our addictions or our codependence, and that our life has become unmanageable, we will "continue to commit them." The first step of the twelve steps of Alcoholics Anonymous (AA) may be the hardest, especially for all who love positions of power or control. Here are the twelve steps of AA, with the word addiction put in place of "alcohol"

1. We admitted we were powerless over addiction—that our lives had become unmanageable.

2. Came to believe that a power greater than ourselves could restore us to sanity.

3. Made a decision to turn our will and our lives over to the care of God as we understood Him.

4. Made a searching and fearless moral inventory of ourselves.

5. Admitted to God, to ourselves, and to another human being the exact nature of our wrongs.

6. Were entirely ready to have God remove all these defects of character.

7. Humbly asked Him to remove our shortcomings.

8. Made a list of all persons we had harmed, and became willing to make amends to them all.

---

net/go/codependency (accessed on July 16, 2014). The term "relationship addiction" is taken from this website.

221. See http://psychcentral.com/lib/symptoms-of-codependency/00011992 (accessed July 10, 2014).

222. Gregory, *Pastoral Rule*, 184.

9. Made direct amends to such people wherever possible, except when to do so would injure them or others.

10.Continued to take personal inventory, and when we were wrong, promptly admitted it.

11.Sought through prayer and meditation to improve our conscious contact with God as we understood Him, praying only for knowledge of His will for us and the power to carry that out.

12.Having had a spiritual awakening as the result of these steps, we tried to carry this message to addicts, and to practice these principles in all our affairs.[223]

When I was a youth pastor, I got to know a teenager who was recovering from drug addiction. When he took his third step, he could only turn his will and life over to the care of HP, the name he gave to his higher power. He told me that God seemed too religious and judgmental, but he was cool with HP. Gregory probably sounds religious and judgmental to some in the twenty-first century when he writes, "those who bewail their sins but do not forsake them should be advised to acknowledge that they will appear before the eyes of the strict Judge . . ."[224] Yet Gregory presents ancient wisdom to help us overcome addictive ways of living. When we begin to accept that we are not the center of the universe, and when we acknowledge there is a Higher Power before whom we will appear, we consider our lives differently, and begin stepping along the path towards healing. As Gregory writes, they "set their steps of their heart toward righteousness."[225]

Codependent people also need roadside assistance. When I broke down along the freeway last year, I pulled out my cell phone, got out my AAA card, and called for roadside assistance. Too often, codependent people live in denial of any problems in their life, and fail to realize how much they are broken down in codependency. Thankfully, God is "merciful and gracious, slow to anger and abounding in steadfast love."[226] God loves to bring healing to our soul diseases "with medicinal antidotes so that we who have departed from him . . . might return."[227] God loves to help all

223. Smith and Wilson, *The Big Book*, 59.
224. Gregory, *Pastoral Rule*, 184.
225. Ibid., 185.
226. Psalm 103:8.
227. Gregory, *Pastoral Rule*, 186.

"who have fallen by losing ourselves," affirms Gregory, lifting up our lives that we "may rise by controlling in ourselves even that which is lawful."[228]

Therefore, all who are bowed down with the burden of addiction or codependence, hear beautiful news: "A broken and contrite heart, O God, you will not despise."[229] When we bring our broken-down, hurting hearts to God, we are washed and lifted out of the mud. There is great hope and help for our inner being to be healed of sickness as well as the unhealthy desire to return again and again to that mess. As we set the steps of the heart towards a new, whole way of living, we are wise to start living "one day at a time," seeking out a mature sponsor or mentor, and welcoming the support of such groups as Alcoholics Anonymous or Al-Anon to encourage us along the way as we learn to "stop living in the problem and begin living in the answer."[230]

CHAPTER 52

The Boastful and the Hypocrites

I went to grad school for three years in Pasadena, California. On New Year's Day, we would join half a million others along the parade route through downtown Pasadena to watch the Rose Parade, with its grand floral floats, marching bands, and pageantry. For two years I was employed by the grad school to stay up all night before the Rose Parade guarding chairs in a seating section along Colorado Boulevard. It was then that I discovered the parade before the parade. From midnight to dawn before the Rose Parade, people cruise the boulevard in their cars, playing loud music, looking for action, showing off, and living loudly in the dark.

Like the midnight parade, there are some boastful souls who love to go on a night ride, parading their lifestyles before others. Like the daytime parade, there are other souls who hide their faults in full view, presenting

228. Ibid.
229. Psalm 51:17.
230. Smith and Wilson, *The Big Book*, 552.

beautiful pageantry before others by pretending to be better than they really are. Gregory is concerned about troubles in both parades.

With the boastful, mentors are wise to help them see that their lives influence others negatively. "If they are unable to eradicate their wickedness, they should at least not allow it to grow in others."[231] Mentors learn to ask good questions. What kind of influence do you hope to have upon others? How does your life help others at this time? Mentors encourage self-examination, helping mentees step outside themselves to have a clearer look at their way of life from an alternative perspective.

People who love to parade their corrupt ways of living may get caught in a destructive cycle of boastful words leading to brash actions leading to arrogant thoughts leading to more boastful words and actions. "He comes to think that his behavior is acceptable, which sinks him ever further."[232] When someone loses "the firm restraint of fear," they no longer "even seek to hide [their] sinful behavior."[233] Instead, they go on parade through the midnight of the soul, blasting their music and lifestyle for all to see and hear without consideration of the unhealthy impact they are having upon others.

On the other end of the spectrum, beneath every glorious daytime parade float rolling by on New Year's Day at the Rose Parade, you will discover people hidden away underneath the flowers, operating those floats. Many of these folks are tired from staying up all night getting these beautiful floats ready for the parade, and they struggle with multiple troubles of their own. We are wise to consider the people beneath the parade floats. Instead of bringing their lives out into the light of day, they build elaborate and beautiful structures to present to the world a false front behind which to hide.

Hypocrisy is an ancient Greek word describing the mask used in Greek theater. Hypocrites wear masks. Most of us have learned to live behind masks. We outwardly project an image of our personality which does not represent our true self. Thomas Merton describes this way of living behind masks in *New Seeds of Contemplation*: "Every one of us is shadowed by an illusory person: a false self. We are not very good at recognizing illusions, least of all the ones we cherish about ourselves."[234]

231. Gregory, *Pastoral Rule*, 187.
232. Ibid.
233. Ibid.
234. Merton, *New Seeds of Contemplation*, 34.

According to Gregory, the way out of the midnight parade of arrogance or the daytime parade of hypocrisy is through self-examination and confession, especially with the help of a soul mentor guiding us. Thomas C. Oden, professor of theology and ethics at Drew University writes of Gregory's vision for wholeness: "At a broad level of generalization, Gregory's pastoral care sought to nurture . . . an appropriate balance of excellent behaviors without the self-deception that invites vice to parade as virtue."[235] As we allow our souls to be illumined, our lives will be purged of self-deception and brought into the light of understanding, opening new possibilities for new ways of living in wholeness. As Merton asserts,

> The only true joy on earth is to escape from the prison of our own false self, and enter by love into union with the Life who dwells and sings within the essence of every creature and in the core of our own souls.[236]

CHAPTER 53

The Impulsive and the Willful

In 1970, two Stanford University psychology professors, Walter Mischel and Ebbe Ebbesen, conducted their famous marshmallow experiment on ninety-two preschool children ages three to five. The test was simple: a single marshmallow was placed in front of the child, and the child was told that they could eat the marshmallow if they wanted, but that they would be awarded a second marshmallow if they waited and the first marshmallow is still there when the adult returned. The adult then left the room, leaving the child alone with the single marshmallow for approximately fifteen minutes. In longitudinal studies conducted twenty years later, the same children who waited for a longer duration before eating the first marshmallow tended to

235. Oden, *Care of Souls in the Classic Tradition*, 56.
236. Merton, *New Seeds of Contemplation*, 26.

cope better in adolescence, performed better in school, and were less likely to use drugs during their teenage years.[237]

We are impulsive and willful creatures. The command center overseeing our impulses and will is located in our frontal lobes, specifically in our prefrontal cortex. In this area of our brain, vital activities for our health and well-being take place, including planning, organizing, impulse control, inner supervision, perseverance, attention, learning from mistakes, and self-monitoring. Those who have suffered injuries to their frontal lobes face such problems as procrastination, poor organization, problems with short-term memory, short attention spans, impulse control problems, poor judgment, and lying.[238]

According to David Masur, director of neuropsychology at Montefiore Medical Center in New York City,

> The frontal lobes distinguish us from lower-order creatures. We have larger frontal lobes, and these are what really are responsible for much of what we define as human behavior, social interaction, ability to plan, organize, some language ability, abstract reasoning or thinking. Much of our society is based on the concept of not only free will but also 'free won't,' the inhibition of response. . . . Maybe down the line somebody can develop a drug or hormone or transmitter system that targets that particular area of brain which strengthens the ability to negate responses which are too impulsive.[239]

Masur raises excellent questions, which come from a better understanding of our frontal lobes: how can we learn better inhibition of our responses, especially regarding impulsive behaviors? How might we strengthen our ability to say no to responses which are too impulsive? How does a person develop self-control? Can we learn to better regulate our impulses without becoming overly controlling with our will?

Gregory considered such questions in the late sixth century, knowing the importance of balance between impulsive and willful ways for healthy

---

237. Walter Mischel, Ebbe B.Ebbesen, and Antonette Raskoff Zeiss, "Cognitive and attentional mechanisms in delay of gratification," *Journal of Personality and Social Psychology* 21, no. 2 (February 1972) 204–218. See http://psycnet.apa.org/journals/psp/21/2/204/ (accessed July 16, 2014).

238. See www.centerforbrain.com/files/Course.section2.neurophysiology.basics.pdf (accessed July 16, 2014).

239. Quoted from http://abcnews.go.com/Health/Healthday/story?id=4508400& page=1#.UdtEf22y2So (accessed July 16, 2014).

living. He was concerned about "those who are overcome by unexpected desires and those who bind themselves deliberately in sin."[240] The impulsive need help recognizing "that they are daily engaged in the war of the present life and to protect the heart, which is not able to protect against wounds . . ."[241] Immediate, daily support and heart protection are required for impulsive people who are easily wounded. Why heart protection? "If the heart lacks anxious caution, it exposes itself to wounds."[242] Those who lack inner strength or self-control need mentors who will support them and protect them, or they will continue to subject themselves to many wounds in body, mind, and soul. Gregory calls this battle a "dark contest," in which the impulsive are wise to "fortify themselves in the fortress of the mind with continuous vigilance."[243]

Gregory returns in this section of *Pastoral Care* to one of his favorite metaphors, that of a ship at sea. "You will be as one who sleeps in the middle of the sea and as a captain who falls asleep and lets go of the rudder."[244] We all have an internal rudder which helps us guide our lives. Some fall asleep, and find themselves like Gregory's sleepy captain, neglecting to "concern himself with the motion of the vices that flow upon him like steep waves."[245] As mentors, we step into a person's life, as though boarding a ship at sea, and assist a mentee in learning to "hold tight to the rudder," and thus "steer the ship directly against the waves or let them come from the side as necessary."[246]

The willful have a different problem. Though they "hold tight to the rudder," some direct their course intentionally into dangerous reefs. "Sins that are bound by deliberation are more slowly resolved," writes Gregory, because when the willful fall into sin after seriously considering better alternatives, "they typically sink into despair."[247] As you read this, you may think of unhealthy areas of your life which you've sought to bring under better control, but you keep choosing to engage in those behaviors or thought

---

240. Gregory, *Pastoral Rule*, 189.
241. Ibid.
242. Ibid.
243. Ibid.
244. Ibid., 190.
245. Ibid.
246. Ibid.
247. Ibid., 191.

patterns. Why do we keep choosing what we know is unhealthy? St. Paul wrestled with this life question long ago:

> I do not understand my own actions. For I do not do what I want, but I do the very thing I hate. . . . For I do not do the good I want, but the evil I do not want is what I do. . . . Wretched man that I am! Who will rescue me from this body of death? Thanks be to God through Jesus Christ our Lord![248] [249]

Just as we are designed with an inner command center to assist us in these matters for our well-being, so a good mentor comes alongside the impulsive and the willful to assist them in learning to grow the fruit of self-control. As Gregory wisely instructs, "So too when the mind vigilantly governs the soul, it suppresses some things directly and avoids others by forethought. In this way, it overcomes immediate dangers through toil and by foresight gathers strength against future obstacles."[249]

CHAPTER 54

Molehills and Mountains

Imagine three different pictures: a river, a ship at sea, and a healthy human body. Rain floods the river, overflowing the riverbanks. Water leaks into the bilge of the ship at sea. A life-threatening rash spreads on the skin of the healthy body. In all three pictures, the change occurs slowly and at first goes unnoticed. Yet small, steady action may bring about major transformation: a river floods, a ship sinks, a body becomes sick. Gregory paints these pictures to describe little troubles which bring about great troubles in the human soul.

Allow me a fourth familiar picture in the form of a proverb: making mountains out of molehills. The small mound of dirt in our front lawn thrown up the night before by a mole is vastly different than the snow-capped mountain in the distance. There are some who indulge in little molehill troubles over and over again. Others avoid the pesky, daily, little

248. Romans 7:15, 19, 24–25.
249. Gregory, *Pastoral Rule*, 190.

faults, but get caught up in major disasters of the soul. These two people need to be mentored differently.

Though little troubles may seem insignificant at first, "when an untold number of them take control, it destroys the life of the body as completely as a single deep wound to the chest."[250] The book of Ecclesiasticus states it this way: "He who spurns small things falls little by little."[251] Gregory believed that multiple minor troubles can present greater danger than one major soul problem, simply because "a minor sin is believed to be nothing at all and so it is retained with a worse result because it continues unabated with little notice."[252] Seawater slowly leaking into a ship at sea presents as much if not more threat to the ship as an immense single wave crashing over her bow.

There are others who "don't sweat the small stuff,"[253] but occasionally tumble into a deep pit and find it impossible to climb out without assistance. Gregory encourages mentors to help mentees "take careful notice of themselves, for while their heart is elated from its preservation against minor sins, it becomes devoured in the moment of their pride by more egregious offenses."[254] Most of us know the stories of the television celebrity preachers who denounced the sins of others year after year, warning their viewing audiences of the pitfalls of sin, only to fall into those grave sins themselves, bringing an end to their ministry and disgrace to their reputations. When I hear someone rant against a minor issue in society, I wonder if it is a major issue within that person's soul. Jesus calls such leaders "blind guides," who "strain out a gnat but swallow a camel!"[255] If we fail to discern between mountains and molehills, how will we be able to help a person distinguish between lessor and greater soul troubles? Better to keep the great vision of faith before our eyes. "The weightier matters of the law: justice and mercy and faith,"[256] are like corrective lenses helping us to see the depths of the river of the soul, or the bilge of the ship of the soul, and thus be more prepared to diagnose the condition of the body of the soul. As

250. Ibid., 192.
251. Ibid.
252. Ibid., 193.
253. Carlson, *Don't Sweat the Small Stuff*, title.
254. Gregory, *Pastoral Rule*, 193.
255. Matthew 23:24, quoted in Gregory, *Pastoral Rule*, 194.
256. Matthew 23:23.

Mother Teresa simply put it, "We can do no great things, only small things with great love."[257]

CHAPTER 55

Starting and Finishing

Every summer over the past decade, our family has enjoyed a week-long backpacking adventure in a national park. In 2013, we hiked into the back-country of Yosemite National Park. In spring of 2013, I sent in our advanced registration for this hiking trip, including the number in our party, our trailhead entrance and exit, and the number of days we planned on being away. The National Park Service wanted to know when we would start hiking and what day we expected to finish. Our time in Yosemite was one of the most spectacular backpacking experiences of my life. We started from the Glacier Point trailhead, hiked a sixty-mile loop around the Clark Range, including over Red Peak Pass at 11,200 feet elevation, and finished eight days later at Happy Isle trailhead in Yosemite Valley, just as we had planned six months earlier.

Just like the National Park Service, Gregory is also concerned about how we start and finish our soul journeys. There are some who "do not begin good works." There are others who "begin but complete few of them."[258] There are many reasons why some people do not step out in faith. Gregory includes ten obstacles common to people who fail to start on their journey into love and growth, including those who have been ruined, those who have fallen down, those who have been wounded, those who pursue what is empty, inexperience, those who focus on what passes away, those who are in pain, those who are afraid, those who hold onto what is false, and those who have had their lives uprooted. Such forces keep us from beginning something new. We find ourselves frozen, numb, and unable to decide what to do.

---

257. Mother Teresa, quoted in Stearns, *The Hole in Our Gospel*, 277.
258. Gregory, *Pastoral Rule*, 194.

The first thing to do with such immobilized people is to help them see the state of their soul, as painful as this may be at first. "They should be told to destroy those things that occupy them destructively."[259] The example Gregory gives is the conversion of Saul of Tarsus. As a powerful and zealous religious leader, Saul was bent upon persecuting the newly birthed church, including officially presiding over the stoning death of Stephen. Before he could begin a new life and career as an apostle, he needed a great light to shine upon him to show him the state of his soul. Saul was blinded on the road to Damascus, when "the bright light came from heaven upon him," and he "did not hear immediately what good it was that he should do but first heard what he had done wrong."[260] When Saul asked God, "Lord, what do you want me to do?" he was told, "Arise, go to the city, and it will be revealed to you what you are to do." Because he was blind, he was led into the city of Damascus, humbled from his position of power and pride before he could be built up to begin anew. Gregory offers an edifying picture of this movement of the soul in the cutting down of trees to be used as beams in the roofs of great buildings.

> We cut down the tallest trees of the forest, so that we might lift them to the roof of the building. But note that these trees are not placed immediately on top of the foundation. For the wood must first be dried (for the moisture is a defect) by laying it flat; only later can it be lifted to the highest parts.[261]

Once the obstacles have been identified and tended to for a time, a person becomes ready to be "lifted to the highest parts." Thus we come upon another soul concern: that of completing the good things we've begun. Just as a runner sets his heart upon the finish line, so we are wise to keep the final goal in mind.

Mirroring the ten obstacles mentioned above, Gregory provides ten goals for each of those who have had difficulty beginning. First, those who have been ruined are to be rebuilt, and after some time they will be able to invest their lives in building up others. Second, those who have fallen down are to be lifted up and encouraged to help lift up others who fall. Third, the wounded are to seek healing, that they may bring wholeness to others who are wounded. Fourth, when a person realizes their emptiness, they can truly begin to be filled with new purpose, and thus become able to help fill

259. Ibid.
260. Ibid., 196, where Gregory quotes from Acts 9.
261. Ibid., 196.

others. Fifth, the inexperienced begin to seek training, apprenticing themselves to wise mentors who will provide good experiences to mature them.
Sixth, a mentor may help turn a mentee away from what is transitory and
turn them toward what endures. Seventh, pain may be transformed into
pleasure when "suffering produces endurance, and endurance produces
character, and character produces hope . . ."[262], so we can learn to celebrate
those places of pain for what they can produce within our soul. Eighth, fear
may lead us to a deeper awareness of our frailty, bringing about a maturing
of trust and an invitation into a life of delight. Ninth, when we let go of what
is false, we open our hands and hearts to learn to hold onto what is true.
Tenth, the places where we've been uprooted may be replanted and grow
new life and health.

When such work takes place in the soul, a person has greater potential
to reach her final destination. But we must strive with great energy towards
the final goal. As Gregory puts it when painting his picture of the soul,

> the human soul in this world is like a ship sailing against the cur-
> rent of a river—it is never able to stay in one place, because it will
> slide back to the lowest area, unless it struggles mightily. There-
> fore, if the strong hand of the one laboring does not complete the
> good works it has begun, the very relaxation of labor will fight
> against what was previously achieved.[263]

CHAPTER 56

Dr. Jekyll and Mr. Hyde

In 1886, Robert Louis Stevenson published his novella *Strange Case of Dr.
Jekyll and Mr. Hyde,* a story first inspired by one of Stevenson's dreams.
While pondering the duality of human nature, including the interplay of
good and evil within the human soul, Stevenson had a dream. As his wife
narrates,

262. Romans 5:3–4.
263. Gregory, *Pastoral Rule,*197.

In the small hours of one morning, I was awakened by cries of horror from Louis. Thinking he had a nightmare, I awakened him. He said angrily: "Why did you wake me? I was dreaming a fine bogey tale." I had awakened him at the first transformation scene.[264]

In Stevenson's tale, Gabriel John Utterson, a London lawyer, investigates unusual events in the life of his friend, Dr. Henry Jekyll, involving an evil man named Edward Hyde. Stevenson's story has entered into our common way of thinking about complex personalities, with "Jekyll and Hyde" referring to a person who is sometimes good and sometimes bad. Gregory understood this soul sickness long ago, when he wrote of "those who do evil secretly and good publically, and those who conceal the good they do, yet allow a bad opinion of themselves because of some of the things they do publically."[265] As Thomas Oden writes, "Gregory grasped clearly the inner complementarity of virtues and vices and was fascinated by their accompanying self-deceptions."[266]

There are those who perform good works outwardly for show while hiding their corrupt hearts behind "self-deceptions." Perhaps you know such a person or can relate to such a soul condition. Most of us identify, at least in part, with Jekyll's condition. Yet, who wants to reveal the real condition of their heart before others? Most of us hide behind a public self. We invest lots of energy in our waking hours keeping that public self looking good and well-groomed. The greater the gap between our public self and our inner, real self, the more dissonance we experience within our soul. Those who have lived with this duality for years may not even realize there is an abyss staring them in the face every time they look in the mirror. Like Stevenson, our night vision is clearer, and our dreams often reveal dark shadows of truth that continue to trouble our sleep. When the characters in our dreams are dramatically different than our waking self, as is often the case, we may want to pay more attention to the state of our soul.

I've had repetitive dreams of working as a road construction boss, wearing a hard hat, and overseeing hundreds of employees building a new freeway. I've never worked in construction. I know nothing about building roads. But at the time, I was pondering moving my family across the nation to pursue a whole new career. Those dreams were paving the way for my soul to head out along the newly built freeways of the heart into a

---

264. Balfour, *The Life of Robert Louis Stevenson*, 15–16.

265. Gregory, *Pastoral Rule*, 198.

266. Oden, *Care of Souls in the Classic Tradition*, 56.

new calling. I've known people who have had repetitive dreams which have haunted them for years, with strange shadowy figures leading them further and further into a mystery—until they realized the truth about what they'd been hiding. As Jesus once declared,

> . . . you are like whitewashed tombs, which on the outside look beautiful, but inside they are full of the bones of the dead and of all kinds of filth. So you also on the outside look righteous to others, but inside you are full of hypocrisy and lawlessness.[267]

Once we bring our hidden soul secrets, including our "bones of the dead," out into the light of wise counseling or mentoring, these troubling dreams fade like morning mist and once again we may sleep in peace.

Those who spend too much effort grooming their public self, according to Gregory, "should be advised to consider how quickly human judgments pass away."[268] Though our contemporary culture is too often driven by ratings, polls, and public opinion, our souls do not need to depend upon the fleeting fancies of human judgments. When we base our self-worth upon the opinion of others by investing significant time and energy into our public image at the neglect of our soul, we overlook the more important matters of the heart. Better to "fix the eyes of [our] mind on the end of things, when the testimony of human praise passes away, and the heavenly sentence, which penetrates every hidden thing, intensifies. . ."[269] As the ancient psalmist declared, "I will meditate on your precepts, and fix my eyes on your ways."[270] Where we focus our eyes determines where we meditate with our souls. If we center our attention on passing fads and fancies, our souls will flit from opinion to opinion, never sure what to believe. When we fix our eyes on the unchanging ways and precepts of eternity, our souls will truly find rest and restoration.

On the other side of the Jekyll and Hyde story are those who "conceal the good works they do, yet allow for a bad opinion of themselves because of some of the things they do publically."[271] There are some who "live virtuously by righteous actions,"[272] yet, spend much energy of the soul

267. Matthew 23:27–28.
268. Gregory, *Pastoral Rule*, 198.
269. Ibid., 199.
270. Psalm 119:15.
271. Gregory, *Pastoral Rule*, 199.
272. Ibid., 200.

hiding their good works out of false humility, afraid of being praised or seen as virtuous. There are many stories in the history of religion of people withdrawing from human society to focus more attention upon the heart and soul. In some of these holier-than-thou groups an attitude of pride or self-righteousness may come upon the members who have withdrawn, as they look down upon secular society as corrupt and filthy. The very people who live virtuously yet hide their good works may end up allowing a bad opinion of themselves to form among others simply out of failure to shine the light of their good works.

The trouble here lies in the motives within the human soul. When we do good works mainly to win praise, our good works turn to dust. But when we do good works out of our love for God or our love for others, they will shine like gold and help motivate others to live better lives. As Gregory asserts, "a good work can be done secretly even though it is performed publically, and again, it can be done publically even when it is secretive."[273] The difference is the motive of the heart. Some do not seek their own glory; others lust for the praise of others. Only when we discover both Jekyll and Hyde living within, and with the help of wise mentoring, can we come to a better understanding of our own dual nature. Then we begin to grow with integrity in our soul and begin to step out of the shadows into the light. As Jesus encouraged, "In the same way, let your light shine before others, so that they may see your good works and give glory to your Father in heaven."[274]

CHAPTER 57

Man on Wire

A few years ago, my wife and I watched the 2008 award-winning British documentary *Man on Wire*, which tells the story of Philippe Petit's high-wire walk between the Twin Towers in New York City. On August 7, 1974, just after seven in the morning, Petit made history by stepping

273. Ibid., 201.
274. Matthew 5:16.

onto a three-quarter-inch wire stretched across the 200-foot gap between the Twin Towers. For the next forty-five minutes he would cross that wire eight times, dancing high above the sidewalks of Manhattan, balancing his life 110 stories above the morning commuters. The Port Authority Police Department arrested him when he finally stepped off the wire, but later released him. All formal charges against him were dropped, but Petit was asked to perform for children in Central Park, which he did by walking on a wire suspended across Belvedere Lake. The key to Petit's success was his amazing sense of balance, developed over years of practice. While walking between the Twin Towers, he carried with him a twenty-six-foot-long balancing pole weighing fifty-five pounds, helping him keep his balance in such an extraordinary place as a quarter mile above the heads of amazed onlookers. One of the police officers, Sgt. Charles Daniels, described what he saw that day:

> I observed the tightrope "dancer"—because you couldn't call him a "walker"—approximately halfway between the two towers. And upon seeing us he started to smile and laugh and he started going into a dancing routine on the high wire. . . . And when he got to the building we asked him to get off the high wire but instead he turned around and ran back out into the middle. . . . He was bouncing up and down. His feet were actually leaving the wire and then he would resettle back on the wire again. . . . Unbelievable really. . . . Everybody was spellbound in the watching of it.[275]

Keeping our balance is no easy task. Many forces in our world today threaten to unbalance our lives or knock us off our feet. What helps you stay in balance? What balancing pole do you hold onto as you step out each day onto the wire? Mentors help their mentees learn to walk a balanced life, as a "man on wire." As a monk, Gregory knew about living a well-balanced life. Australian Benedictine monk Michael Casey describes "the principle of complementarity" that Gregory offers in his *Pastoral Care:*

> To every virtue there is a corresponding opposite that is itself also a virtue. Pastoral discernment is a matter of knowing which end of the polarity to recommend to a particular person at a particular time. The Middle Way enunciated by Benedict attempts to capture the benefits of opposite virtues while minimizing their liabilities. This is the much-praised Benedictine "balance"—remembering

275. Quoted from http://www.pbs.org/wgbh/americanexperience/features/biography/newyork-tightrope/ (accessed July 16, 2014).

of course that balance always requires the creative interaction of
two opposed forces; it is never the single-minded pursuit of an
extreme.[276]

Gregory offers many examples of this balanced way of mentoring by helping people learn to live in a healthier balance: between humility and pride;
between laziness and impetuosity; between impatience and lack of zeal; between frugality and prodigality; between marriage and celibacy; and even
between the lesser good and the greatest good. We encourage humility to
the proud "in a way that does not increase the despair of the timid," while at
the same time building the confidence of the timid "in a way that does not
increase the pride of the arrogant."[277] We instruct the lazy to do good deeds,
"in a way that does not increase the immoderate action of the impetuous,"
while challenging the hasty to show moderation and restraint "in a way that
does not encourage listless security of the idle."[278] We encourage "bountiful
charity" among the frugal, "but not in a way that loosens the restraint of
the prodigal"; while offering the gift of self-control to the prodigal, "but
not in a way that increases the withholding of possessions by the thrifty."[279]
Marriage is to be honored and encouraged, but not to the neglect of the gift
of celibacy; while purity is to be praised among the celibate, but "not in a
way that leads the married to despise the flesh."[280] The greatest good is to
be elevated "in a way that does not ignore lesser goods"; while those same
lesser goods are welcomed, but "not in a way that compromises the greatest
goods."[281] Thomas Oden writes of Gregory's sense of balance:

> Virtue was thought to be an appropriate balance of desirable be-
> haviors. But Gregory was keenly aware that any excellent balance
> that is capable of being achieved is capable also of being easily up-
> set in one direction or another, toward either an excess or a deficit,
> which is the essential definition of *vitium*, or *vice*.[282]

Maintaining excellent balance in an imbalanced world demands the help
of mentors, both formal and informal, to walk with us and teach us how

276. Casey, *An Unexciting Life*, 133–134.
277. Gregory, *Pastoral Rule*, 202.
278. Ibid.
279. Ibid.
280. Ibid.
281. Ibid., 203.
282. Oden, *Care of Souls in the Classic Tradition*, 56.

to step with balance, lest we get "easily upset in one direction or another." One of the key works of a good mentor, according to Oden, "involves sorting out the layers of self-deception that prevent one from seeing these imbalances."[283]

Gregory describes such mentoring as "a two-edged sword,"[284] referring to an image from the book of Hebrews. "Indeed, the word of God is living and active, sharper than any two-edged sword, piercing until it divides soul from spirit, joints from marrow; it is able to judge the thoughts and intentions of the heart."[285] By holding onto Scripture, our two-edged sword, we will be able to "judge the thoughts and intentions of the heart," keeping our balance as we walk with others in an unbalanced world. Again, Michael Casey comments on the ancient way of balanced living:

> The means which Benedict proposes is a balance between different sorts of activity: *ora et labora*, between physical and spiritual tasks, between solitude and community, between conservation and progression, between human and divine. Benedict has the typically Roman abhorrence for extremes—even in good things. Everything is to be done in moderation. . . . Every value is balanced by its complement. Even contemplation is not sought as an end in itself, but only as an aspect or dimension of a life progressively given over to God.[286]

CHAPTER 58

Hopelessly Optimistic[287]

I like oxymorons. Some of my favorites include: alone together, virtual reality, absolutely unsure, eschew obfuscation, instant classic, nonworking mother, cheerful pessimist, and hopeless optimist. Oxymora make good

283. Ibid., 56.

284. Gregory, *Pastoral Rule*, 202.

285. Hebrews 4:12.

286. Casey, *An Unexciting Life*, 107.

287. This chapter combines chapters 37 and 38 of Part Three of *Pastoral Rule*.

bumper stickers, like the one I saw recently: "Thank God I'm an atheist!" Even the word *oxymoron* is an oxymoron, meaning "sharp fool." We can see that Gregory was a sharp fool for his time when he warns mentors to "be aware of the hidden impulses and motivations of individuals and to turn with skill from one person to another, like a gymnast turns from side to side." The ancient art of soul mentoring recognizes the oxymoronic quality of the human soul, with conflicting opposites at work, requiring the unique skill of turning from "side to side," as we seek to offer help to "a person who is a slave to contrary passions," helping people with the strange mixture within their souls, and moving towards a more balanced way of living centered in God. Soul mentoring requires, as Thomas Oden writes,

> . . . a sensitive and subtle balance between caring for the person's inward feeling process, and caring for the person's outward behavioral change . . . taking practical steps toward implementing constructive changes in order that a more richly grounded happiness may become possible.[288]

Mentors step into the civil war going on in the human heart between "contrary passions" and out-of-balance behaviors. Some forces draw us upward into the light of love; others lead us downward into the cellar of darkness. The care of contrary souls includes walking alongside people as they step upward towards wholeness or passionately trip downwards into destruction. Sometimes a person goes one step up and two steps down. Other times, a person will take two backward steps, but turn around and make three forward steps into maturity. "It is often the case that one who can be too joyous can just as easily become dangerously depressed when sadness suddenly springs upon him."[289] Mentors learn to care for souls with moderation, even in the face of extreme swings of motives and actions.

Gregory views mentors as "physicians of souls," encouraging friends, pastors, teachers, coaches, parents, and caregivers to mentor others with "skillful discernment," helping people find "medicine for the soul."[290] In medical practice, doctors and nurses triage patients according to the severity of their symptoms and required care, making careful assessment of the wounds requiring the most attention. In mentoring, we are wise to take time to triage, discerning with mentees the various symptoms and care needed to bring about health and wholeness. Gregory writes that "it is often

288. Oden, *Care of Souls in the Classic Tradition*, 57.

289. Gregory, *Pastoral Rule*, 203.

290. Ibid.

the case that when two vices attack the same person, one oppresses him more lightly and the other more severely."[291] The lesser trouble sometimes needs to be overlooked to deal directly with the more dangerous problem. In doing so, a mentor helps to rescue "the life of the one infected, thus enabling him to find a more fitting time to administer the [spiritual] medicine for the lesser fault as well."[292] Through all troubles, true soul mentors offer mentees the gift of hope, and even in the face of great suffering and despair, we are wise to focus upon the potential in all people to heal and grow into full maturity and wisdom. When it comes to the possibilities that lie within every human soul, I love those cheerful pessimists, but personally, I tend to be hopelessly optimistic.

CHAPTER 59

Milk and Meat

We enter this life drinking our mother's breast milk. The first mentoring we encounter in life, while breastfeeding during the first few months after we are born, are with our mothers and fathers. Sometime during our first year of life, our parents begin to introduce us to other types of food, and slowly we are weaned from a milk-only diet. Scientific studies have shown conclusively that breast milk provides such excellent nutrition for a baby that it is the only food and drink a baby needs for the first six months of life. Many mothers breastfeed their babies until their first birthday. Since I am married to a public health nurse who specializes in lactation and breastfeeding, I've learned about the amazing gift of breast milk for babies. In *Breastfeeding and Human Lactation,* breastfeeding experts Jan Riordan and Karen Wambach call human milk "the gold standard for infant nutriment," asserting that "the nutritional components of human milk, combined with its immune and anti-allergic properties, make it the ideal foundation for optimal infant health."[293] The longer mothers are able to breastfeed their

291. Ibid., 204.
292. Ibid.
293. Riordan and Wambach, *Breastfeeding and Human Lactation,* 150.

babies, the better the outcome for those babies, including boosting the baby's immune system, lowering the baby's risk of cancer, increasing the baby's capacity to learn, decreasing future dental troubles, reducing the risk of childhood obesity, and decreasing the likelihood of childhood diseases such as asthma and diabetes.

As we grow up, we learn to eat many kinds of food and to drink many kinds of drinks besides milk. The same holds true with the life of the soul. At first, mentors are wise to keep the mentoring diet simple and nutritious, offering mentees the milk of wisdom and loving-kindness, drawing from Scripture's life-giving drink to grow the soul. In this way, Paul wrote to the people of ancient Corinth:

> And so, brothers and sisters, I could not speak to you as spiritual people, but rather . . . as infants in Christ. I fed you with milk, not solid food, for you were not ready for solid food. Even now you are still not ready, for you are still of the flesh.[294]

Gregory refers to Paul's instructions above, encouraging mentors to wait until the right season to offer "the proper portion of words, so that it will not be wasted on a heart that is unable to hold it."[295] There is no use hurrying growth or force-feeding a person heavy food they will not be able to hold down. A mentor "should realize that [she] should not draw the souls of [her] listeners beyond their strength."[296] Some mentees are not yet ready to be given solid food, for they are still too immature, and need time to grow before they are ready to digest meatier types of soul nutrition.

CHAPTER 60

Footprints and Pathways

Many of the greatest stories ever told view life as a journey home, including Homer's *Odyssey*, Jesus's parable of the Prodigal Son, Tolkein's *The Lord*

294. 1 Corinthians 3:1–3.
295. Gregory, *Pastoral Rule*, 206.
296. Ibid., 205.

of the Rings, Frank Baum's *The Wizard of Oz,* and Maurice Sendak's 1964 Caldecott-award-winning picture book *Where the Wild Things Are.* Gregory, like his soul mentor Benedict, understood mentoring as two people walking home together along paths of the heart. Benedict wrote in the closing pages of his famous guidebook, concerning our soul journey,

> Are you hastening toward your heavenly home? Then with Christ's help, keep this little rule that we have written for beginners. After that, you can set out for the loftier summits of the teaching and the virtues we mentioned earlier, and under God's protection you will reach them.[297]

As a monk, Gregory was deeply influenced by *The Rule of St. Benedict,* writing his own mentoring guidebook to encourage beginners to learn the "art of arts." In the closing pages of Gregory's *Pastoral Care,* he writes, "In the midst of these considerations, we are brought back in the zeal of charity to what we have already said, which is that every [mentor] should be 'heard' more by his deeds than by his words."[298] Both Benedict and Gregory call us to a life of charity and integrity, a life in which we are heard "more by our deeds than by our words." Both call us to follow the way that leads to God and everlasting life. They did this first by their way of life, and then through their words and writings.

We mentor others first by the wisdom of our lives, not primarily by the wisdom of our words. "Let [us] first perform lofty deeds and then convince others to live well."[299] Mentoring is about helping others to live well. Soul work happens best when mentees see this wellness in the lifestyles of their mentors. "Let [us] carefully examine whether there is anything about [our lives] that is sluggish and, if so, correct it with strict observance. Only then should [we] tell others how to live their lives."[300] What is sluggish in your soul at this time? How often do you take time to carefully examine your own soul? With whom are you meeting for such careful examination? If we neglect this primary work of self-examination, how can we hope to help

---

297. Chittister, *The Rule of Benedict,* 301.

298. Gregory, *Pastoral Rule,* 206–207. I've replaced Gregory's term "preacher" with "mentor" to include other mentors including counselors, therapists, spiritual directors, coaches, parents, and friends.

299. Ibid., 207.

300. Ibid.

a mentee examine their life? "Before [we] offer any words of exhortation, [we] should proclaim by [our] actions everything that [we] wish to say."[301]

I live a few blocks from the Pacific Ocean. When walking along the beach, sometimes I follow footprints left in the sand, walking a while in someone else's steps. I must make adjustments to my stride to keep in step with that unknown person who came before me. I shorten my stride to step with children, and lengthen my stride to keep up with a runner's footprints. In the same way, mentors and mentees walk together, stepping in one another's footprints. As Gregory writes, "Moreover, the footprint of his good living should be that path that others follow rather than the sound of his voice showing them were to go."[302] What does good living look like in the twenty-first century? Seek out the paths from ancient times and discover wisdom to follow in this good way.[303]

This book presents a practical manual for the soul, for mentors and mentees alike, offering Gregory's ancient footprints to follow, step by step. For centuries now, Gregory's path has been mostly forgotten. Those who walk in his steps will discover a pathway leading to healthy, wise living. Gregory calls us into a life of soul mentoring drawn from his own life experience as he followed in the footprints of his mentor who walked before him. Gregory's mentor, St. Benedict, describes soul mentoring as a journey we take together along sacred paths across a lifetime.

> As we progress in this way of life and in faith, we shall run on the path of God's commandments, our hearts overflowing with the inexpressible delight of love. Never swerving from God's instructions, then, but faithfully observing God's teaching . . . until death, we shall through patience share in the sufferings of Christ that we may deserve also to share in the eternal presence. Amen.[304]

Mentoring Inventory: Second Half of Part Three

Here at the end of Part Three of *Soul Mentoring*, I invite you to take a few moments to review Gregory's guidebook on spiritual formation,

301. Ibid.

302. Ibid.

303. My previous book, *Ancient Paths*, follows the path offered by St. Benedict in *The Rule of St. Benedict*, encouraging contemporary readers to "walk in the ancient paths" of Benedictine spirituality today.

304. Chittister, *The Rule of Benedict*, 21.

considering ways you may deepen your life and develop greater wisdom for mentoring. Below, I invite you to participate in a final mentoring inventory, drawn from the second half of Part Three of Gregory's *Pastoral Care*. As in the inventory from the first half of Part Three, this inventory also requires taking three steps of self-examination.

Step One: For each of the twenty pairs in Part Three, mark an X along the continuum between each pair, identifying the place along this spectrum which most accurately describes your life and character. Go back into Part Three to review any pair of opposites which may not be clear to you.

Step Two: For each of the pairs below, mark a star along the spectrum between these opposites, identifying the place where you'd like your life to grow in the future.

Step Three: Look over the pairs below and write in the space below any notes or impressions which come to mind as you review your life in light of these personality types and the potential growth for your life in the future.

41. Giver--Taker

42. Thrifty---Wasteful

43. Quarreler---------------------------------------Peaceable

44. Sower of Discord----------------------------Sower of Peace

45. Ignorant--Proud

46. Hesitant---Hasty

47. First---Last

48. Married---Single

49. Sinner--Saint

50. Active--Contemplative

51. Addiction-----------------------------------Codependence

52. Boastful--Hypocritical

53. Impulsive---Willful

54. Molehills-------------------------------------Mountains

55. Starting---Finishing

56. Dr. Jekyll---Mr. Hyde

57. Balanced-------------------------------------Imbalanced

58. Optimist---Pessimist
59. Milk--Meat
60. Footprints--Pathways

Conclusion: Care of the Soul of a Mentor— Portrait of a Master Artist

One of my favorite painters, Rembrandt (1606–1669), launched his early career as a successful portrait painter in Amsterdam, Holland. Throughout his life, he also loved to paint his own image, completing nearly a hundred self-portraits in oil paintings, etchings, and sketches. Over the span of forty years, looking into a mirror for hours at a time, Rembrandt painted himself in nearly every decade of his life, from the playfulness of youth, to the melancholy of middle age, to the wisdom of old age. Though so many self-portraits may seem a bit narcissistic, consider also what an excellent idea it is to study your own face as it changes through the decades.

Like Rembrandt, Gregory the Great also painted human portraits, as evidenced when he wrote in his epilogue: "Alas, I am like a poor painter who tries to paint the ideal [person]."[1] Gregory attempted something much more challenging than portraits of human faces. In *Pastoral Care*, he sought to paint a portrait of the human soul in all its complexity, imbalance, immaturity, and splendor.

Gregory wrote his *Pastoral Care* as a personal letter to John, the Bishop of Ravenna, Italy, one of his mentees. During his fourteen years as pope, Gregory wrote hundreds of letters to people he was mentoring across Christendom.[2] In his first year as pope, he wrote *Pastoral Care*, written initially as a personal letter, but ultimately intended as a guidebook for all who were involved in soul mentoring, both as mentors and mentees.

In his opening words of *Pastoral Care*, Gregory writes to John: "You reprove me, beloved brother, with a kind and humble intention, for having hoped that by hiding myself I might flee the burdens of pastoral care."[3] The final paragraph of Gregory's lengthy letter closes with another personal ad-

1. Gregory, *Pastoral Rule*, 212.
2. Copies of 854 of Gregory's letters have been preserved.
3. Gregory, *Pastoral Rule*, 27.

dress to John, the first recipient of Gregory's guidebook on soul mentoring: "Behold, good man, being compelled by the necessity of your request, I have tried to show what the qualities of a spiritual director ought to be."[4]

Throughout *Pastoral Care*, we see Gregory's deft brush strokes, as he seeks to bring greater definition to soul mentoring, not as an abstract idea, but as a personal practice between two friends. Pastoral care, spiritual direction, counseling, parenting, teaching, coaching, and mentoring share the same common foundation: a caring relationship between two people.

In the conclusion of *Pastoral Care*, also known as Part Four, Gregory illuminates his canvas with concern for the self-care of the mentor. "It is necessary that great care be taken. . . . Otherwise, the one who is able to return others to health will ignore himself."[5] Nobody wants to be treated by a sick doctor or a mentally ill counselor. Unless a mentor takes good care of herself, the very act of seeking to bring others to health may cause harm to a mentor's well-being over time. "Let [her] not abandon [herself] by helping others or stumble as [she] enables others to rise."[6] It may come as a surprise to some that helping others towards health may be harmful to your own personal well-being. Anyone who has spent a few years in a people profession knows stories of burn-out, brokenness, and tragic failure among those who have invested their lives and souls in serving others.

In my profession of pastoring, statistics for burnout are not encouraging. On average, pastors last four years at any particular church, and only fourteen years in their pastoral career before stepping out of ministry. One third of pastors are burned out within their first five years of ministry. I was part of that statistic in my first five years of pastoral service. 60 percent of pastors admit they would leave their profession if they had somewhere else to go. 75 percent of pastors struggle with mental or emotional troubles such as severe stress, alienation, anger, or depression. 80 percent of pastors believe that pastoral ministry negatively impacts their life and family. 90 percent of clergy say they are unqualified or inadequately prepared for their vocation. Clergy, doctors, and lawyers struggle with substance abuse, addiction, and suicide more than any other profession. Every month, 1,500 clergy leave their pastoral ministry in the United States due to burnout or other problems.[7] In his book *An Unhurried Life*, pastor Alan Fadling tells

4. Ibid., 212.

5. Ibid., 209.

6. Ibid.

7. See http://www.barnabasministriesinc.org/86-front-page-articles/8-what-pastors-

a story about a South American tribe who walked long distances together, and then suddenly stopped and sat down together. When asked why they did this, they simply answered, "they needed the time of rest so their souls could catch up with them."[8] Pastors, teachers, counselors, spiritual directors, and other mentors also need regular times to stop and rest so our souls can catch up.

A few years ago, I attended a course taught by the Covenant Church titled "Vocational Excellence," offered to men and women involved in full-time professional pastoral care. One of the most arresting statements made by the instructor was "neglect of self-care is a form of clergy misconduct." We spent the week learning about practical approaches to self-care, including professional counseling, spiritual direction, mentoring, support groups, accountability with peers, weekly personal time away from work for rest, the weekly rhythm of work and rest, and creative time for refreshment and renewal, among other strategies for self-care to keep us from burning out or flipping out. Everyone taking the class was required to take a series of personality inventories, such as the Myers-Briggs, the Enneagram, and the Thomas Kilman Conflict Mode Instrument. We all met with a professional counselor to assess our soul health and discover better approaches to self-care. Personally and professionally, I found this class of great benefit for my own self-care and personal growth to strengthen my life as a soul mentor and pastor.

The connection between self-care and mentoring others is essential in our day, but not new. Gregory wrote about these truths fourteen centuries ago in *Pastoral Care*, encouraging mentors to "consider carefully" who they are. "To this end," Gregory adds, "when you penetrate the highest things, you will still recognize that you are human, and when you are seized into the heights, you will be recalled to yourself by the anxiety of your infirmity."[9] Are you taking time to "carefully consider" who you are? How often do you take personal inventory of your soul in the midst of caring for others? How aware are you of your humanity? How in touch are you with your anxieties or your infirmities? The better we know the person in the mirror, including

face-today; http://www.pastorburnout.com/pastor-burnout-statistics.html; http://faithandleadership.com/programs/spe/articles/200601/critical.html (accessed July 11, 2014).

8. Fadling, *An Unhurried Life*, 15.

9. Gregory, *Pastoral Rule*, 211.

our limitations and troubles, the better we will be able to reach out to care for the souls of others.

I love the spirit of the Holstee Manifesto, written by Holstee founders Dave, Mike, and Fabian in 2009: "Ask the next person you see what their passion is, and share your inspiring dream with them. . . . Life is about the people you meet, and the things you create with them so go out and start creating."[10] This world needs more dreamers, lovers, and creators. Too often, we encounter discouraging obstacles that get in the way of pursuing such an encouraging vision of life. Many soul troubles rise up within us or threaten us from the outside. In his epilogue, Gregory mentions many soul troubles, including, "swelling of pride," self-neglect, stumbling, arrogance, "the state of sluggishness," self-flattery, self-deception, corruption "through countless vices," "desire to be admired," "lust for praise," and "anxiety of infirmities." I hope this list of troubles does not describe your soul. If it does, help is readily available even in the face of such limitations. The great Mentor of our soul loves to help us grow in love, faith, and hope. God desires to bring health to others through us who suffer from soul troubles. In the very places where we are wounded, we can find comfort and strength to help others in their sufferings. Paul, a man who went through intense suffering on behalf of those he mentored, writes an amazing vision of caring for others out of the very consolation he received from God.

> Blessed be . . . the God of all consolation, who consoles us in all our affliction, so that we may be able to console those who are in any affliction with the consolation with which we ourselves are consoled by God. For just as the sufferings of Christ are abundant for us, so also our consolation is abundant through Christ. If we are being afflicted, it is for your consolation and salvation; if we are being consoled, it is for your consolation, which you experience when you patiently endure the same sufferings that we are also suffering.[11]

The word consolation, which comes up nine times in this one paragraph, can also be translated as "comfort," a mentoring word in Greek which literally means to be "called alongside" another person.[12] God comes alongside us to mentor us in our troubles, comforting and consoling us, and then calls us alongside others who are being afflicted, to bring God's gift of comfort

10. See http://shop.holstee.com/pages/manifesto (accessed July 11, 2014).

11. 2 Corinthians 1:3-6.

12. The Greek is *parakaleo; para* (alongside), *kaleo* (called).

and soul mentoring in the face of their suffering. The late Henri Nouwen called this type of mentor a "wounded healer."[13] In his book by that title, first published in 1979, Nouwen wrote about people involved in pastoral care. In this Nouwen quote, I've substituted the word "mentor" for "minister," and "mentoring" for "ministry."

> The [mentor] is called to recognize the sufferings of his time in his own heart and make that recognition the starting point of his own service. Whether he tries to enter into a dislocated world, relate to a convulsive generation, or speak to a dying man, his service will not be perceived as authentic unless it comes from a heart wounded by the suffering about which he speaks. Thus nothing can be written about [mentoring] without a deeper understanding of the ways in which the [mentor] can make his own wounds available as a source of healing.[14]

One of my favorite paintings by Rembrandt is his seascape, *The Storm on the Sea of Galilee,* painted soon after he arrived in Amsterdam in 1633, when he was twenty-seven years old. In the painting, followers of Jesus struggle for dear life in a boat crossing the Sea of Galilee. The boat is thrust upward upon a threatening wave, surrounded by dark storm clouds, while the crew attempts to take down the sails, hold onto the rudder, and wake up their Lord. Jesus is just waking up in Rembrandt's painting, looking upon the life-threatening situation with calm eyes and a peaceful soul. Gregory's *Pastoral Care* closes with this same picture, one of his favorite metaphors for our life journey, that of a sailing ship crossing the sea. In Gregory's painting, he sees his life as a ship tossed "back and forth by the waves," and he asks for help from his mentee to lift him up with his prayers.

> I am trying to point others to the shore of perfection, as I am tossed back and forth by the waves of sin. But in the shipwreck of this life, I beg you to sustain me with the plank of your prayers, so that your merit-filled hands might lift me up, since my own weight causes me to sink.[15]

May you too find your way to the "shore of perfection" as you seek out the help of a soul mentor who will sustain you, lift you up, and journey with you through many storms and calm seas to your journey's end. Like

13. See Nouwen, *The Wounded Healer.*
14. Nouwen, *The Wounded Healer,* xvi.
15. Gregory, *Pastoral Rule,* 212.

Gregory, I too ask you to sustain me with the plank of your prayers, grateful you've taken time to journey with me through these pages, as we press onward in the adventure of soul mentoring.

APPENDIX A

The Life and Legacy of Gregory the Great

Listen! Your watchmen lift up their voices.

~ISAIAH 52:8[1]

I love learning the meaning of people's names and believe the meaning of one's name has potential power to shape one's life. My middle name, Gregory, comes from the Greek word *gregoreo,* meaning "to keep watch," a word Jesus spoke to his followers as a life command.[2] In the ancient world, watchmen were a key part of civil defense, standing alert through the night upon the city walls to detect the coming of any threats from the outside. Today, we still employ watchmen in many forms, including night patrol officers, security guards, TSA agents, the Coast Guard, and technological watchmen such as firewalls, antivirus software, and caller ID.

Gregory (540–604) stood on watch in the late sixth century, looking over the crumbling Roman Empire with eagle eyes, lifting up his voice as a watchman while overseeing the lives of many in his care. I offer in this essay a brief overview of Gregory's life and legacy, that you may better understand Gregory in light of the times in which he lived, and the impact his life had upon generations who followed his example of soul mentoring.

On a personal note, my parents gave me the name Gregory in 1957, though it took half a century before that gift began to be unwrapped and lived out in my life. The year I turned forty-nine, in 2006, I became a Benedictine oblate at Mount Angel Abbey in Oregon, and I took Gregory as my oblate name. Benedictine oblates are invited to take on an oblate name

---

1. New International Version.

2. In Greek, the command "keep watch," is a single word, *gregoreite.* See Matthew 24:42 and 25:13.

141

in honor of one of the great heroes of faith, as encouragement in this new way of life and faith. I chose the name Gregory in honor of Gregory the Great, seeking to learn from his life and writings mentoring for my soul.[3] That same year, I began to study Gregory's book, *Pastoral Care*. My first introduction to this classic work on the ancient art of caring for others was Thomas Oden's excellent survey, *Care of Souls in the Classical Tradition*.[4] Oden presents Gregory as a model for soul mentoring, surveying the impact Gregory had upon western civilization throughout his life as a monk, pope, administrator, musician, theologian, but supremely as a mentor of souls. When elected bishop of Rome in 590, Gregory's first order of business was to write *Liber regulae pastoralis*, "the book of pastoral guidance," commonly known as *Pastoral Care*.

Studying Gregory's book on mentoring has been something like stumbling upon a long-abandoned gold mine. Over the past few years, I've cautiously stepped into the darkened tunnels of this work, exploring various paths in this ancient labyrinth of mentoring. The discovery of buried riches of wisdom for soul care in Gregory's writings has caused me to want to put up a new a sign outside this old work declaring, "Gold mine back in operation!" For a millennia, from the late sixth century well into the sixteenth century, *Pastoral Care* was the most popular mentoring manual among spiritual leaders across the Roman Empire, an ancient gold mine of practical wisdom for soul care. Thomas Oden writes that Gregory's work became "a standard handbook of pastoral care for subsequent generations" after Gregory's death. Oden boldly declared Gregory's book to be "the most widely read single text in the history of pastoral care."[5] Until the time of the Protestant Reformation, Gregory's mentoring manual was the one book given to all newly ordained priests across Christendom, a handbook for spiritual formation in the early years of ministry. For nearly a thousand years, Gregory's "golden little book" truly was the gold standard for pastors in developing the ancient art of soul mentoring.[6]

Gregory was born into a wealthy Roman family in AD 540. Though he was sheltered in childhood from many of the disruptive influences in

3. For more information on becoming a Benedictine oblate, see http://www.osb.org/obl/index.html (accessed on July 14, 2014).

4. See Oden, *Care of Souls in the Classic Tradition*.

5. Ibid., 49 and 54.

6. Biographer F. Homes Dudden calls Gregory's *Pastoral Care* the "golden little book." See Dudden, *Gregory the Great*, 228.

society around him, Gregory grew up in troubled times, with the city of Rome overthrown by foreign conquerors several times during his earliest years. Gregory was ten years of age at the time of Benedict's death in 550, a death that occurred at Monte Cassino Abbey, just fifty miles south of Rome, where Gregory lived. In later years, Benedict became a major influence upon Gregory as spiritual father and soul mentor through his writings, instructing him in the ancient art of mentoring according to *The Rule of St. Benedict*.

As a young man, Gregory studied law and became involved in Roman politics. At age thirty-three, he was appointed prefect of Rome, the highest civil office in the city. Soon thereafter his father died, leaving Gregory an inheritance of several estates. At the age of thirty-four, in 574, after a time of deep spiritual crisis, Gregory took the radical step of giving his wealth to the poor and taking up vows of stability, conversion of life, and obedience as a Benedictine monk within the new Benedictine movement. He transformed his estates into monasteries, including a Benedictine monastery in Sicily and another at the family estate in Rome, which became St. Andrew's Abbey. Gregory loved the contemplative life within the cloister, though this quiet way of life was only to last four years.

In 578, Pope Pelagius II ordained Gregory as deacon and sent him as papal ambassador to Constantinople, hoping to win political support from that influential eastern city for help against military troubles facing Rome. For nearly seven years, Gregory lived and served with other fellow Benedictine monks in what is now Istanbul, Turkey. Though his mission to Constantinople was mostly unsuccessful, he learned to balance the contemplative life and active life during those years, leading a monastic community while engaging in political diplomacy. In the morning he stepped out of the cloister to enter the active life of diplomacy. In the evening, he stepped off the busy streets of Constantinople to retired once more into the contemplative life within the cloister. During these years, he wrote a lengthy commentary, *Morals on the Book of Job*.

Upon his return to Rome in 585, he devoted his life once more to the care of souls as abbot of his beloved community at St. Andrew's Abbey. In 586, Gregory became secretary and personal assistant to the ailing Pope Pelagius II, a position he held until 590, the year Pelagius II died. Multiple troubles besieged the city of Rome during these years, including a failing economy, the threat of foreign invasions, and a plague which spread through the city and killed thousands of her citizens. At this critical time in history, at the age of fifty, Gregory was unanimously elected to the papacy. The papacy was not new to Gregory's family, with a great-great-grandfather and a distant uncle both having served in that high office. But Gregory flatly refused the position, preferring to sit like Mary at the feet of Jesus in contemplative service to God rather than face the Martha-like distractions of active service to humanity. Gregory even wrote to the Roman emperor, begging him not to confirm the election. After months of persuasion and prayer, and with some hesitancy, Gregory was consecrated as bishop of Rome on September 3, 590, the first monk ever to be elected Pope.

In the fourteen years he served as bishop of Rome, Gregory dramatically reformed the office of the papacy, unveiling his genius as a spiritual leader in such diverse realms as administration, ecclesiastical reform, liturgical music, care for the poor, financial management, world missions, preaching, and writing. But the greatest gift Gregory offered the world was his wisdom in the care of souls. Gregory chose as his title *servus servorum Dei,* "servant of the servants of God," a title initiated by Gregory and carried by popes to this day. Gregory's choice of this new title was likely inspired by the words of Jesus.

> But Jesus called them to him and said, "You know that the rulers of the Gentiles lord it over them, and their great ones are tyrants over them. It will not be so among you; but whoever wishes to be great among you must be your servant, and whoever wishes to be first among you must be your slave."[7]

Gregory was the first biographer of Benedict, having published his work on the life of Benedict in 593, just four decades after Benedict's death.[8] The life of Benedict and *The Rule of St. Benedict* deeply influenced Gregory's vision and practical wisdom of pastoral care. Gregory chose to call his manual for mentoring *Liber regulae pastoralis,* or "Book of Pastoral Rule," a title influenced by Benedict's manual for communal spiritual life, known in Latin simply as *Regula.* The Latin word *regula,* usually translated as "rule," refers to a measuring tool, such as a ruler, yardstick, or measuring tape. *Regula* can also mean "pattern" or "guiding principle." Though George Demacopoulos translates the title of Gregory's book as *The Book of Pastoral Rule,* as mentioned in the Preface, I prefer the title *Pastoral Care,* and read Gregory's book as a practical handbook for spiritual mentoring, thus avoiding the

7. Matthew 20:25–27.

8. The story of Benedict's life, including reference to *The Rule of St. Benedict* is found in book two of Gregory's collection of four books known as *Dialogues.*

legal connotation of "rule" as law or regulation. Gregory and Benedict were both less concerned with rules, and more concerned with measurable growth in the spiritual lives of individuals and communities.

Throughout Gregory's *Pastoral Care* we hear echoes of Benedictine spirituality, including such basic patterns for spiritual growth as balance, loving accountability, Christlike service, humility, silence, spiritual guidance, moderation, and meditation upon Scripture. Like Benedict, Gregory loved describing soul mentoring with such metaphors as medical practice, shepherding, journeying together, and gardening.

Gregory's *Pastoral Care* rapidly spread across Christendom. Gregory first sent his book north to Ravenna, to John, the archbishop of that city, the person addressed in the opening letter of *Pastoral Care*. "Gregory, to the Most Reverend and Holy Brother John, a Fellow Bishop: You reprove me, beloved brother, with a kind and humble intention for having hoped that by hiding myself I might flee the burdens of pastoral care."[9] He also sent his manuscript to England, along with *The Rule of St. Benedict*, carried by Augustine, a monk from St. Andrew's Abbey and leader of the first missionary band sent by Rome to England.[10] Three hundred years later, Gregory's work was translated into Old English under the orders of King Alfred the Great, becoming one of the earliest manuscripts written in the English language. In an attempt to unify the training of priests and bishops across Christendom, Gregory had copies of his *Pastoral Care* sent across the European continent, including to Leander, Archbishop of Seville, who spread it among the churches in Spain; and also to Maurice, emperor of the Byzantine Empire from 582–602, who had Gregory's work translated into Greek for use in his realms.

Alcuin, the great English scholar during the time of Charlemagne, wrote to the archbishop of York about Gregory's handbook in AD 796: "Wherever you go, let the handbook of the holy Gregory go with you. Read it, and re-read it often. It is a mirror of the pontifical life and a cure for every wound inflicted by diabolical deceit."[11] In 813, Charlemagne ordered that Gregory's book be given to all bishops at their consecration, "and they were admonished, and solemnly promised, to observe what was written therein

9. Gregory, *Pastoral Rule*, 27.

10. Augustine of Canterbury (d. 604), "the apostle to the English," was sent by Gregory as a missionary to England in 597, and is to be distinguished from Augustine of Hippo (354–430).

11. Dudden, *Gregory the Great*, 239.

in their life, their teaching, and their decisions."[12] According to medieval historian Bertram Colgrave, "The *Regula Pastoralis*, or *Pastoral Care*, was also a very popular book in England. Bede, writing to Egbert, Archbishop of York, urged him to make use of it . . . for his private meditations. Alcuin constantly recommended it. . . . It is a book which had much influence all through the Middle Ages"[13] Within a few centuries, Gregory's guidebook for soul mentoring became the leading manual for soul care across the European continent, shaping the pastoral role across ethnic, linguistic, and social boundaries for a millennium.

> One of the most significant contributions of Gregory's work was the solidification of an image already within the tradition and destined to influence pastoral theology for the remainder of the medieval period. For Gregory, the work of the pastor was the "art of arts" and its practice likened to the care of the physician, whose knowledge and actions contributed to the healing of the body.[14]

By the time of the Protestant Reformation, Gregory's manual for soul mentoring could be found all across Europe, in nearly every ecclesiastical library, read by most priests and bishops, and used as the standard for pastoral care and soul mentoring across Christendom. As biographer Frederick Dudden, who also served as chaplain to King George V and King Georg VI, wrote of the widespread impact of Gregory's *Pastoral Care*.

> The maxims of Gregory have molded the Church. They have sensibly shaped the conduct and the policy of the Church's rulers, and as a modern writer well expresses it, have "made the bishops who have made modern nations." The ideal which Gregory upheld was for centuries the ideal of the clergy of the West, and through them the spirit of the great Pope governed the Church, long after his body had been laid to rest beneath the pavement of St Peter's.[15]

Strangely, Gregory's *Pastoral Care* is mostly overlooked in our time, a book that is rarely read today except by seminary professors and students of early church history. Translations into English have been few and far between. To find one prior to the most recent 2007 translation by George Demacopoulos, we must go back to Henry Davis's 1951 English translation, and then

12. Ibid.
13. Colgrave, *The Earliest Life of Gregory the Great*, 29–30.
14. Shinners and Dohar, *Pastors and the Care of Souls in Medieval England*, 2–3.
15. Dudden, *Gregory the Great*, 240.

to the late nineteenth century to find previous translations into English. While Demacopoulos's edition provides a helpful sixteen-page introduction, it lacks textual notes and commentary to help a twenty-first-century reader understand Gregory's ancient wisdom.

When I first read Gregory's book on soul mentoring in 2006, the idea came to me to bring Gregory's writing forward into the twenty-first century, to make his wisdom accessible to a whole new generation of mentors, counselors, coaches, teachers, priests, pastors, and spiritual directors. I believe Gregory offers our century the ancient wisdom we need to find balance and rest for our own soul through the ancient practice of soul mentoring, and thus, we will be better equipped to make our world a better place, one person at a time. As medieval historian C. Warren Hollister writes,

> [Gregory's] real genius lay in his keen understanding of human nature and his ability as an administrator and organizer. His *Pastoral Care*, a treatise on the duties and obligations of a bishop, is a masterpiece of practical wisdom and common sense. It answered a great need of the times and became one of the most widely read books in the Middle Ages.[16]

16. Hollister, *Medieval Europe*, 62–63.

APPENDIX B

Study Guide for Individual or Group Study

When hiking in the wilderness of our national parks, my family and I occasionally come upon solo hikers. On a recent hike, we met a woman in her twenties on the final day of a fifty-mile solo trek. I admired her confidence and tenacity in hiking alone, but also grieved for her, that she had no one to share the joys and burdens of the trail along the way. She was grateful for our companionship during the brief hours we spent alongside her in camp.

I believe God designed us to grow together alongside others who are also growing. We are meant to walk together. The following study guide is written for either individual or group use. Perhaps the best use of this study guide is to find a mentor or friend who is willing to meet with you weekly. Share answers to the following questions from each chapter as you seek together to grow your life with God in your journey toward your heavenly home.

Introduction: When Setting Out on a Long Journey

- What motivated you to enter into soul care? If you are serving in pastoral ministry, what were some of the motives for entering this ministry? If you are involved in informal, personal mentoring of others, what initially got you interested in this kind of service?
- What burdens weigh the heaviest upon you in your service of caring for souls, or in pastoral ministry?
- In what way has your growth in soul mentoring or pastoral ministry been "step by step"? What were some of the steps?
- Who has been of greatest help mentoring you as you began to mentor others?

Part One: The Journey into Mentoring— Learning the Art of Arts

Chapter 1

- Think of some skill you've learned by taking lessons from an expert. What were some of the best ways that expert imparted their knowledge to you?

- What does intensive study mean to you? Describe one of the hardest classes you've ever taken.

- How do you choose a doctor? How do you choose a spiritual mentor? What is similar and what is different?

- Which of the various metaphors for mentoring make most sense to you in your thinking about mentoring: an art studio with master-apprentice relationship; a medical clinic with doctor-patient relationship; a farm and field with shepherd-sheep relationship; or a journey with guide-hiker relationship?

Chapter 2

- If you have trained in formal classroom studies for your work in mentoring, how effective was your formal education in preparing you to care for souls?

- What is your view of degree programs in soul care such as graduate degrees in pastoral care or spiritual formation?

- Remember a time when you were very thirsty. How does the metaphor of thirst help you better understand the soul needs of others?

- Name three ways we can help people find good drinking water for their souls.

Chapter 3

- If offered a multimillion-dollar contract for a "reality" television show, how do you think you would respond?

- What are your thoughts about adversity? In what ways do you try to avoid suffering?
- When is it wise to embrace suffering and when is it masochistic to do so?
- How can we better care for the inner life of another by being willing to suffer with them in the places where their hearts hurt?
- What does it mean to you to walk in the footsteps of Jesus?

Chapter 4

- If you have ever stood or walked at the edge of a very high cliff, recall how you felt at that place, and how you changed your way of life there. What does such a place have to teach us about soul mentoring?
- How do you maintain a healthy balance between externals and internals? How do you balance caring for the lives of others and caring for your own life? How do you keep from being distracted by many things and focusing upon the one thing most important?
- How easy or difficult is it for you to turn away from televisions, cell phones, and computers? How easy or difficult is it for you to turn fully toward the life of one person?
- What is your inner compass in mentoring? What map or guidebook do you follow?

Chapter 5

- What would you consider to be the seven most important character traits for excellence in soul care?
- What gifts, including personal talents or spiritual gifts, have you been given?
- How would you help someone discover their gifts and bring them out into the open where they can be shared with someone in need?
- How will you shine your light this week?

Chapter 6

- What hesitations do you have in caring for the soul of another? What obstacles are in your life right now that hinder you in bringing health and growth to someone else?

- What is your definition of humility? How did you respond to the definition offered in this chapter?

- Think of a time when you knew you needed to help someone but avoided doing so. What kept you from stepping forward?

- How has sacred composting worked in your life?

Chapter 7

- What are some of the honest reasons you entered into soul care? If you are in full-time ministry, describe your sense of vocational call. What motivated you to enter your profession?

- What unhealthy motivations do you find within your soul at this time? What do you do about these motives?

- Study the vocational callings of Moses (Exodus 3), Isaiah (Isaiah 6), and Jeremiah (Jeremiah 1) to find encouragement in your work of soul care.

- Who do you have in your life at this time who can help carry your soul burdens? How often do you unburden your mind and heart to this person?

Chapter 8

- Who has mentored you? Who taught you the art of guiding souls? From whom have you received soul care and a good example of how to practice soul care?

- Which of the examples of soul care mentioned in this chapter were most helpful to you: soul care as a high and noble task; soul care as a master artist with an apprentice; soul care as overseeing another; or soul care as Mary Poppins with Jane and Michael Banks?

- Review the list from 1 Timothy 3:1–2. Which quality best represents your life at this time? Which quality is most out of reach for you at this time?

- Consider the ancient soul care balance mentioned in this chapter. Which side of the scale do you tend to favor or lean towards more heavily? Praise or correction? Encouragement or exhortation?

Chapter 9

- Think of a time you've been at sea in rough weather. How seasick did you get? How did you weather the storm? How much help were you to others during that storm?

- What storms have you faced in your spiritual life? What storms, including mental, emotional, and spiritual ones, have you weathered over the past decade?

- What is your understanding of the virtue of humility? How can a person acquire humility? How can arrogance be deflated in our souls?

- What are your thoughts about John Newton's story? How has the song "Amazing Grace" influenced you or encouraged you?

Chapter 10

- Recall a time when you were very thirsty. How might that physical experience help you better relate to the spiritual condition of others?

- Which of Gregory's twelve ways for watering thirsty souls makes most sense to you? Which seems most unfamiliar or strange?

- What changes do you need to make in your way of living to better prepare yourself for spiritual mentoring?

- How have you helped to water an arid heart?

Part Two: The Character of a Mentor— Drinking from Mountain Streams

Chapter 11

- What struggles do you currently face with impurities in heart and mind?

- How do you deal with these? What steps do you take to find inner purity?

- How do you respond to Gregory's image of people as "living vessels"?

- How might you be used to help someone else find purity in their soul?

Chapter 12

- Think of a time you went for a day hike, or perhaps a backpacking trip involving miles of hiking along an unfamiliar trail. What did you do to prepare for this trip?

- What has helped you gain perspective in caring for the souls of others?

- How do you react to someone who obviously lacks integrity, whose words are not matched by their life or character?

- How might you better match your words to your way of living?

Chapter 13

- What types of food are best improved with salt? How much salt do you use in a typical day? What do you think of the metaphor of salt for use of words with others?

- Do you prefer to talk or would you rather listen? Which is harder for you, listening or speaking?

- What is hardest for you about listening? At what time of day do you find it easiest to listen?

- One of the sure marks of a wise mentor is someone well-seasoned and balanced in the practices of silence and speech. How well-seasoned and balanced are you?

Chapter 14

- Think of a time you've stood at a high place, perhaps a mountaintop or maybe just a rooftop, and looked out upon the world. How did that perspective help you return to "street level" later on?

- What is your understanding of contemplation? How do you practice contemplation? How have you learned to contemplate?

- Which of the five steps into contemplation do you find easiest, and which is hardest? 1) Sit still. 2) Breathe. 3) Be aware. 4) Focus. 5) Relax.

- In seeking to live a well-balanced life of contemplation and compassion, both ascending to the heights of contemplation and descending into the valley of compassionate service, what steps will you take with others this week?

Chapter 15

- What are your favorite pictures of your mother and your father? What wisdom or life skills did your parents teach you?

- How are you at balancing gentleness and discipline, grace and truth, or mercy and justice? Which sides of these do you tend to lean most heavily on?

- Bringing together the best wisdom of your parents, what could you share with others about mentoring?

- How do you balance kindness and discipline in your relationship with others, holding them together in the fire of the soul, and forging them into discernment tools to bring about inner growth?

Chapter 16

- Which gets more of your attention, internals or externals? Are you more of an inner-life person or an outer-life person?

- How easy is it for you to ignore the ringing of your cell phone or turn off the television? How often to you interrupt a conversation with a person to attend to some electronic distraction?

- How many minutes or hours each day to you devote to the care of souls, both your own soul and the souls of others? What does this say about how you are balancing your inner and outer lives at this time?

- How might you become more attentive to both physical and spiritual aspects of life, in your own life as well as in the lives of others?

Chapter 17

- What does moderation mean to you as a way of life? In what ways are you living immoderately?

- Ask yourself some hard questions regarding living moderately: Am I out of balance? Am I seeking more to please people or be genuine and truthful? Am I being too harsh with this person, or too lenient? Am I willing to carry the same expectations that I've placed upon the lives of those under my care? How hypocritical am I in my words and in my way of life? Who is holding me accountable and helping me to live with greater integrity at this time? Am I puffed up with knowledge and a sense of self-importance, or am I building others up in love?

- What motivates you inwardly to do what you do when offering soul care to another?

- How are you practicing the great art of moderation, tempering truth with love and seasoning love with truth, so that mentors and mentees alike may know truth and experience love?

Chapter 18

- What are some masks people love to wear today?
- What are some vices masquerading today as virtues (e.g. workaholism)?
- How can we learn to discern? What has helped you develop better discernment?
- Who has encouraged you to grow in boldness, to remove your masks, and learn to discern what lies beneath the masks of other?

Chapter 19

- When was your last medical checkup? When was your last mentoring checkup, during which you allowed your soul to come under the care of a mentor?

- How does the medical metaphor help you better understand the art of soul care in mentoring? In what ways is a mentor like a physician of the soul?

- What is one of your weaknesses, and what are you learning from this weakness?

- If you are currently mentoring another person, how do you assess their inner health, discern core problems, and reveal potential avenues toward health?

Chapter 20

- Think of your favorite place to get a drink of water. Why is it your favorite place?

- How do you refresh your soul?

- What did you learn in this chapter about sacred reading, or *lectio divina*?

- How do you carry soul refreshment with you, and how are you currently helping others quench their inner thirst?

Part Three: The Practice of Mentoring—Becoming a Skilled Musician

- What was most helpful in the two mentoring inventories from Part Three?

- What did you learn about yourself in this section?

- How might this study of opposites influence the way you mentor others, or the way you view mentoring from now on?

- How balanced or out of balance are you right now?

- Review the chapters on the forty pairs of opposites from Part Three, and write out any key concepts you've learned from this section.

Pairs of Opposites   Key Concepts

1. Men and Women
2. Young and Old
3. Poor and Rich
4. Joyful and Sad
5. Leaders and Followers
6. Employees and Employers
7. The Educated and the Uneducated
8. The Bold and the Shy
9. The Assertive and the Timid
10. The Impatient and the Patient
11. The Generous and the Envious
12. The Sincere and the Insincere
13. The Healthy and the Sick
14. The Sensitive and the Hardened
15. The Silent and the Talkers
16. The Lazy and the Hasty
17. The Meek and the Angry
18. The Humble and the Arrogant
19. The Stubborn and the Indecisive
20. The Excessive and the Abstinent
21. Givers and Takers
22. The Thrifty and the Wasteful
23. The Quarrelers and the Peaceable
24. Sowers of Discord and Sowers of Peace
25. The Ignorant and the Proud
26. The Hesitant and the Hasty

Bibliography

Aldington, Richard, ed. *The Viking Book of Poetry of the English-Speaking World.* New York: Viking, 1941.

Anderson, Keith. *Spiritual Mentoring: A Guide for Seeking and Giving Direction.* Downers Grove, IL: IVP, 1999.

Bacovcin, Helen, trans. *The Way of a Pilgrim and The Pilgrim Continues His Way.* New York: Image, 1978.

Balfour, Graham. *The Life of Robert Louis Stevenson,* vol. 2. New York: Charles Scribner's Sons, 1912.

Balsavich, Marion, OSB. *The Witness of St Gregory the Great to the Place of Christ in Prayer.* Rome: Pontificium Athenaeum Anselmianum, 1959.

Batiffol, Pierre. *Saint Gregory the Great.* Translated by John Stoddard. London: Burns Oates & Washbourne Ltd., 1929.

Benedict. *RB 1980: The Rule of St. Benedict in English.* Edited by Timothy Fry. Collegeville, MN: Liturgical, 1982.

———. *RB 1980: The Rule of St. Benedict in Latin and English with Notes.* Edited by Timothy Fry, Timothy Horner, and Imogene Baker. Collegeville, MN: Liturgical, 1981.

Benner, David. *Spiritual Companions: The Gift of Spiritual Friendship and Direction.* Downers Grove, IL: IVP, 2004.

———. *Spiritual Direction and the Care of Souls: A Guide to Christian Approaches and Practices.* Downers Grove, IL: IVP, 2004.

Berry, Wendell. *New Collected Poems.* Berkeley: Counterpoint, 2012.

Bockmann, Aquinata, OSB. *Perspectives on The Rule of Saint Benedict: Expanding Our Hearts in Christ.* Collegeville, MN: Liturgical, 2005.

Borchert, Gerald L. and Andrew D. Lester, eds. *Spiritual Dimensions of Pastoral Care: Witness to the Ministry of Wayne E. Oates.* Philadelphia: Westminster, 1985.

Brandreth, Gyles, ed. *Oxford Dictionary of Humorous Quotations.* Oxford: Oxford University Press, 2013.

Bronwen, Neil, and Matthew Dal Santo, eds. *A Companion to Gregory the Great.* Leiden, Brill, 2013.

Brooke, Christopher. *The Age of the Cloister: The Story of Monastic Life in the Middle Ages.* Mahwah: Paulist, 2003.

Bucer, Martin. *Concerning the True Care of Souls.* Carlisle: Banner of Truth, 2009.

Burns, Bob, Tasha Chapman, and Donald C. Guthrie. *Resilient Ministry: What Pastors Told Us about Surviving and Thriving.* Downers Grove, IL: IVP, 2013.

Carlson, Richard. *Don't Sweat the Small Stuff . . . And It's All Small Stuff.* New York: Hyperion, 1996.

BIBLIOGRAPHY

Carlson, Richard, and Joseph Bailey. *Slowing Down to the Speed of Life: How to Create a More Peaceful, Simpler Life from the Inside Out.* New York: Harper Collins, 1997.

Casey, Michael, OCSO. *Sacred Reading: The Ancient Art of Lectio Divina.* Liguori: Triumph, 1996.

———. *An Unexciting Life: Reflections on Benedictine Spirituality.* Petersham: St. Bede's Publications, 2005.

Cheetham, Nicolas. *Keeper of the Keys: A History of the Popes from St. Peter to John Paul II.* New York: Charles Scribner's Sons, 1983

Chittister, Joan, OSB. *The Rule of Benedict: A Spirituality for the 21st Century.* New York: Crossroad, 1995.

———. *Wisdom Distilled from the Daily: Living The Rule of St. Benedict Today.* New York: HarperCollins, 1990.

Clinton, Timothy, and George Ohlschalger, eds. *Competent Christian Counseling.* Vol. 1: *Foundations and Practice of Compassionate Soul Care.* Colorado Springs: Waterbrook, 2002.

Clinton, Timothy , and Linda Taylor, eds. *The Soul Care Bible: Experiencing and Sharing Hope God's Way.* Nashville: Thomas Nelson, 2001.

Cobb, John B., Jr. *Theology and Pastoral Care.* Philadelphia: Fortress, 1977.

Colgrave, Bertram, trans. *The Earliest Life of Gregory the Great.* Cambridge: Cambridge University Press, 1968.

The Contributors. *The Benedictine Handbook.* Collegeville, MN: Liturgical, 2003.

Dudden, F. Homes. *Gregory the Great: His Place in History and Thought.* New York: Russell & Russell, 1905.

Dykstra, Robert, ed. *Images of Pastoral Care.* St. Louis: Chalice, 2005.

Ellsberg, Robert. *All Saints: Daily Reflections on Saints, Prophets, and Witnesses for Our Time.* New York: Crossroad, 1997.

Fadling, Alan. *An Unhurried Life: Following Jesus' Rhythm of Work and Rest.* Downers Grove, IL: IVP, 2013.

Feiss, Hugh, OSB. *Essential Monastic Wisdom: Writings on the Contemplative Life.* New York: Harper San Francisco, 1999.

Foster, Richard. *Life With God: Reading the Bible for Spiritual Transformation.* New York: HarperCollins, 2008.

Fowler, James W. *Faith Development and Pastoral Care.* Philadelphia: Fortress, 1987.

Frend, W.H.C. *The Rise of Christianity.* Philadelphia: Fortress, 1985.

Gee, Margaret, Ed. *The Dalai Lama. Words of Wisdom: Quotes by His Holiness the Dalai Lama.* Kansas City: Andrews McMeel, 2001.

Gregory the Great. *The Book of Pastoral Rule.* Nicene and Post-Nicene Fathers: Second Series, vol. 12. Translated by James Barmby. Grand Rapids: Eerdmans, 1976.

———. *The Book of Pastoral Rule.* Translated by George E. Demacopoulos. Crestwood: St. Vladimir's Seminary Press, 2007.

———. *Dialogues.* Translated by Odo John Zimmerman, OSB. Washington, D.C.: The Catholic University of America Press, 1959.

———. *The Letters of Gregory the Great, translated with introduction and notes.* Translated by John Martyn. Toronto: Pontifical Institute of Medieval Studies, 2004.

———. *Life and Miracles of St. Benedict.* Collegeville, MN: Liturgical, 1984.

———. *Pastoral Care.* Translated by Henry Davis, SJ. Ancient Christian Writers, vol. 11. Mahwah: Paulist, 1950.

———. *Pastoral Practice:Books 3 and 4 of the Regula Pastoralis.* Translated and edited by John Leinenweber. Harrisburg: Trinity, 1998.

BIBLIOGRAPHY

Guenther, Margaret. *Holy Listening: The Art of Spiritual Direction.* Boston: Cowley, 1992.

Hendricks, Howard, and William Hendricks. *As Iron Sharpens Iron: Building Character in a Mentoring Relationship.* Chicago: Moody, 1999.

Herwegen, Ildephonsus, OSB. *St. Benedict: A Character Study.* Translated by Dom Peter Nugent, OSB. London: Herder, 1924.

Hollister, C. Warren. *Medieval Europe: A Short History.* New York: Random House, 1982.

Holmes, Urban T. III. *Spirituality for Ministry.* San Francisco: Harper & Row, 1982.

Howarth, Sir Henry H. *Saint Gregory the Great.* London: John Murray, 1912.

Hymns for the Living Church. Carol Stream, IL: Hope, 1974.

Jamison, Christopher, OSB. *Finding Sanctuary: Monastic Steps for Everyday Life.* Collegeville, MN: Liturgical, 2006.

Johnson, Eric. *Foundations for Soul Care: A Christian Psychology Proposal.* Downers Grove, IL: IVP, 2007.

Kardong, Terrence G., OSB. *Benedict's Rule: A Translation and Commentary.* Collegeville, MN: Liturgical, 1996.

Kreider, Larry. *Authentic Spiritual Mentoring: Nurturing Believers Toward Spiritual Maturity.* Ventura: Regal, 2008.

Latourette, Kenneth Scott. *A History of Christianity.* Vol. 1, *Beginnings to 1500.* New York: Harper & Row, 1975.

Leclercq, Jean, OSB. *The Love of Learning and the Desire for God.* New York: Fordham University Press, 1974.

Leech, Kenneth. *Spirituality and Pastoral Care.* Cambridge: Cowley, 1989.

Lewis, C. S.. *Mere Christianity.* London: Garden City, 1952.

Louv, Richard. *The Nature Principle: Reconnecting with Life in a Virtual Age.* Chapel Hill: Algonquin, 2011.

Markus, R. A. *Gregory the Great and His World.* New York: Cambridge University Press, 1997.

May, Gerald G. *Addiction and Grace: Love and Spirituality in the Healing of Addictions* .New York: HarperCollins, 1988.

McNeill, John T. *A History of the Cure of Souls.* New York: Harper & Row, 1951.

Merton, Thomas. *The Living Bread.* New York: Farrar, Straus & Cudahy, 1956.

———. *New Seeds of Contemplation.* New York: New Directions, 1961.

———. *Spiritual Direction and Meditation.* Collegeville, MN: Liturgical, 1960.

Meyer, Wendelin, OFM. *The Pastoral Care of Souls.* Translated by the Rev. Andrew Green, OSB. St. Louis: Herder, 1944.

Miller, J. Keith. *A Hunger for Healing: The Twelve Steps as a Classic Model for Christian Spiritual Growth.* New York: HarperCollins, 1991.

Milton, John. *John Milton: Complete Poems and Major Prose.* Edited by Merritt Y. Hughes. Indianapolis: Odyssey, 1957.

Moorhead, John. *Gregory the Great.* London: Routeledge, 2005.

Mullins, Edwin. *Cluny: In Search of God's Lost Empire.* New York: Blue Bridge, 2006.

Niklas, Gerald R. *The Making of a Pastoral Person.* New York: Alba House, 1996

Nolte, Dorothy Law. *Children Learn What They Live.* New York: Workman, 1998.

Nouwen, J. M. Henri. *Spiritual Direction: Wisdom for the Long Walk of Faith.* New York: HarperCollins, 2006.

———. *The Way of the Heart.* New York: Ballantine, 1981.

———. *The Wounded Healer.* New York: Doubleday, 1979.

Oden, Thomas C. *Care of Souls in the Classic Tradition.* Philadelphia: Fortress, 1984.

BIBLIOGRAPHY

———. *Pastoral Theology: Essentials of Ministry*. San Francisco: HarperCollins, 1983.

Okholm, Dennis. *Monk Habits for Everyday People: Benedictine Spirituality for Protestants*. Grand Rapids: Brazos, 2007.

Parrott, Drs. Les and Leslie. *The Complete Guide to Marriage Mentoring*. Grand Rapids: Zondervan, 2005.

Patton, John. *Pastoral Care: An Essential Guide*. Abingdon, 2005.

Pennington, Basil M., OCSO. *Listen With Your Heart: Spiritual Living with The Rule of Saint Benedict*. Brewster: Paraclete, 2007.

Purves, Andrew. *Pastoral Theology in the Classical Tradition*. Louisville: Westminster John Knox, 2001.

Reese, Randy, and Robert Loane. *Deep Mentoring: Guiding Others on Their Leadership Journey*. Downers Grove, IL: IVP, 2012.

Riordan, Jan, and Karen Wambach. *Breastfeeding and Human Lactation*. Sudbury: Jones and Bartlett, 2010.

Robinson, David, *Ancient Paths: Discover Christian Formation the Benedictine Way*. Brewster: Paraclete, 2010.

———. *The Busy Family's Guide to Spirituality: Practical Lessons for Modern Living from the Monastic Tradition*. New York: Crossroad, 2009.

———. *The Christian Family Toolbox*. New York: Crossroad, 2001.

Schutz, Roger. *The Rule of Taizé*. Taizé: Les Presses de Taizé, 1968.

Shinners, John, and William J. Dohar, eds. *Pastors and the Care of Souls in Medieval England*. Notre Dame: University of Notre Dame Press, 1998.

Sister of Notre Dame. *The Life of St. Gregory the Great*. Dublin: Talbot, 1924.

Smith, C. Christopher, and John Pattison. *Slow Church: Cultivating Community in the Patient Way of Jesus*. Downers Grove, IL: InterVarsity, 2014.

Smith, Dr. Bob, and Bill Wilson. *The Big Book of Alcoholics Anonymous*. Lark, 2013.

Stearns, Richard. *The Hole in Our Gospel*. Nashville: Thomas Nelson, 2010.

Stoddard, David. *The Heart of Mentoring: Ten Proven Principles for Developing People to Their Fullest Potential*. Colorado Springs: NavPress, 2009.

Sutera, Judith, OSB, ed. *Work of God: Benedictine Prayer*. Collegeville, MN: Liturgical, 1997.

Swan, Laura, OSB. *Engaging Benedict: What the Rule Can Teach Us Today*. Notre Dame: Ave Maria, 2005.

Thompson, Marjorie. *Soul Feast: An Invitation to the Christian Spiritual Life*. Louisville: Westminster John Knox, 2005.

Tvedten, Brother Benet, OSB. *How to Be a Monastic and Not Leave Your Day Job: An Invitation to Oblate Life*. Brewster: Paraclete, 2006.

Uhlein, Gabriele. *Meditations With Hildegard of Bingen*. Vermont: Bear & Company, 1983.

Vest, Norvene. *Preferring Christ: A Devotional Commentary and Workbook on The Rule of St. Benedict*. Harrisburg: Morehouse, 2004.

Volz, Carl A. *Pastoral Life and Practice in the Early Church*. Minneapolis: Augsburg Fortress, 1990.

Warren, Rick. *The Purpose Driven Life*. Grand Rapids: Zondervan; 2002.

Wicks, Robert J., ed. *Handbook of Spirituality for Ministers*. 2 vols. Mahwah: Paulist, 1995.

Zachary, Lois. *Creating a Mentoring Culture: The Organization's Guide*. San Francisco: Jossey-Bass, 2005.

———. *The Mentee's Guide*. San Francisco: Jossey-Bass, 2009.

———. *The Mentor's Guide*. San Francisco: Jossey-Bass, 2000.